THE BLENDED FAMILY
WORKBOOK FOR TEENS

the BLENDED FAMILY

workbook

for teens

EXERCISES TO HELP YOU MANAGE
YOUR EMOTIONS AND NAVIGATE CHANGE

SONYA JENSEN, LMFT

ROCKRIDGE
PRESS

For general information on our other products and services or to obtain technical support, please contact our Customer Care Department within the United States at (866) 744-2665, or outside the United States at (510) 253-0500.

Rockridge Press publishes its books in a variety of electronic and print formats. Some content that appears in print may not be available in electronic books, and vice versa.

Series Designer: Elizabeth Zuhl
Cover Designer: Sean Doyle
Interior Designer: Catherine San Juan
Art Producer: Hannah Dickerson
Editor: Nora Spiegel
Production Editor: Holland Baker
Production Manager: Riley Hoffman

Illustrations © Anugraha Design/Creative Market
Author photo courtesy of Anna Kraft

Paperback ISBN: 978-1-63807-196-9 | eBook ISBN 978-1-63878-500-2
R0

This Workbook Belongs To:

_____

CONTENTS

INTRODUCTION

Welcome to a workbook designed especially for you, with plenty of space and freedom to process your emotions, thoughts, and needs. The major transition you're experiencing in your family is challenging. You may not know what you're going to get out of this workbook yet, but I hope you'll find it. Regardless of how this book found you, please know that you can take from it what you want and need at any given time. There is no pressure to use all the resources in one go.

My name is Sonya, and throughout the course of my career as a Licensed Marriage and Family Therapist, I have worked with many teens and their families to build better and stronger bonds as they go through life's major challenges and changes. Growing up, my family was blended, too, and I remember how difficult it was for me, my parents, and my siblings to navigate limited time together and big emotions when we were both together and apart. I've written this workbook to create a space where you can feel a little less alone in this world, find hope, and begin to understand who you are, what you want, and how to get it. What you're going through is unique to you, and only you can decide what you need and want from this experience. I hope this workbook will help you feel seen and understood and give you clarity for how you'll move forward as you navigate this transition in your family.

Becoming a blended family means merging two families into one. Blending anything together takes time, patience, and often a lot of grace and mistakes along the way. You and your entire family are trying to figure out what you feel about this new life that is being created, what you want from it, what you don't want from it, and how to pull it all together. This process is often messy and complicated. No two situations are the same, but I'll share some stories with you that might make you feel more hopeful for the future.

Throughout this workbook you will find exercises and journaling ideas that will help you identify your emotions and what you can do with them, as well as clarify your needs and goals for your role in this new family. Most of my clients feel really overwhelmed at the beginning of such a huge transition in their lives and do not even know where to begin. I will help you create strong building blocks that can reduce overwhelm and other intense emotions.

There is no one right way to move through this workbook. I believe that when you need it most, the tools I've included will make their way to you. By that, I mean you may find yourself wanting to work through the whole book in one sitting, or you may be drawn to utilize certain prompts and exercises. You can skip around chapters based on your needs or move through cover to cover. Make this experience your own, and listen to what your heart and mind need in this chapter of your life. This book will be here for you when you need it.

Everyone can benefit from having someone to talk to about life's challenges. I hope this workbook will support you in learning about yourself and sharing what you learn with someone you trust. Please know that asking for help, like talking with a professional therapist or your school counselor, is a sign of strength. While this workbook will be a great support for you, it cannot take the place of a therapist, medication support, and help from a medical professional, if required. You can use the prompts and exercises in this book to spark conversations with the professionals in your life so they can help you dive even deeper into your own experience and find your way through it.

I hope that by the end of this book you feel connected to the stories, optimistic for the future, and a little less lonely in this world. Your experience is unique to you, but there are others out there—online and in your community—who know what it's like to transition into a blended family. The list of resources on page 144 can help you connect with them. Let's get started and see where these pages take us.

The Truth about Blended Families

Going through any major change in your life will cause you to think, feel, and see yourself and the world around you differently. Maneuvering through this change with thoughtfulness, mindfulness, and care can strengthen your sense of empathy, helping you learn to love yourself and others better. In part I, you will explore the change happening to you and around you through helpful prompts and insights. The goal is to learn more about yourself and identify the feelings, hopes, and fears you have before we move on to what to do about them.

There were four of us. My older siblings lived primarily with their father in California, and my sister and I lived with our mom and dad. We'd see one another for long periods of time in the summer and on school holidays. Between our two sets of siblings, we had a 10-year age gap, so connecting and growing as a family was challenging. Us younger siblings wanted to see our older half brother and sister and engage them in our hobbies and interests. When they'd come to visit, our expectations were high, but the amount of interaction was low. It was difficult to understand the new dynamics of our family and why our older siblings didn't want to spend that much time with us. It was easy to take it personally and keep hoping that one day it would change. Blending our families together meant changing what we expected from those relationships. Instead of bonding through hobbies and interests, we bonded through TV shows and movie nights. Our older siblings introduced us to things we hadn't seen before, and it made our time together full of excitement as we grew up. Changing my expectations around the ways we would interact helped me focus on the small but good moments of connection we did have. While our relationship as siblings has stayed relatively distant, when we are together, we laugh about the shows we watched and do impersonations of our parents. Those moments are few and far between, but they matter.

Every Family Has Its Ups and Downs

The idea that everything is going to run smoothly in any family or throughout a transition usually leads to disappointment and frustration. All families, whether blended or traditional, experience challenges. It takes a lot of effort to figure out what does and doesn't work when blending a new family together—or even just being a family in general. It helps to normalize the pain that comes with change. You may be wondering, *Will this ever change? Do things get better, or will I ever feel better about what has happened to my family?* Maybe you're even daydreaming about the day you move out and looking forward to leaving home. When we're upset or frustrated, it's common to use daydreaming as a way to gain some sense of control in a difficult situation. Transitions and uncertainty make it a challenge to remain hopeful and thoughtful about what you need and what you want. Share what is on your mind with the people who make you feel safe. It takes time to figure out all the swirling thoughts and big emotions that come up and to put them into words. Take the pressure off yourself to have everything figured out, and remember that your feelings about this change are normal and worth processing to get to know yourself and your new family better.

A Blended Family Has Particular Challenges

Merging two families into one presents a greater challenge than just moving to a new house or changing schools. Your safe space, your home, has now changed completely. It's possible that you've lost some sense of freedom and consistency in the way you spend your time. You have a new stepparent who is concerned about your well-being. They may have a role in making decisions that impact your life. Maybe you miss what your family used to be like and what you hoped it would still be. The feelings of grief, anger, and helplessness may seem overwhelming. Blending your families may even mean that the relationship you had with a parent has changed and you've lost the time you used to spend together.

NEW DYNAMICS

Your way of life before your parent married or chose to move in with their new partner has changed everything for you. You're trying to figure out what is happening next—and so are your parents. The new dynamic in your home will require a lot of feedback and cooperation to get things working well for everyone.

DIFFERENT VALUES AND PRIORITIES

Values are feelings or things that affect the decisions made in your home. What are the values that used to drive your home and family? For example, strong family connection is a value that might override doing things perfectly. As your family is changing, so are the values and priorities that shape how the members of your family move through life together and make decisions.

HEIGHTENED FEELINGS AND EMOTIONS

You may have felt some anger or deep sadness at some point during your family's transition. You may have even been asked to read this workbook because of how intense your emotions are. Know that with any big change like this, your emotions are bound to be high, and they deserve to be heard and recognized as important to understand.

A Mindfulness Exercise for Difficult Times

A mantra is something you say to yourself that validates what you're feeling and changes how you go about expressing that feeling. My favorite mantra is, *These feelings will come and they will go, as long as I don't assign danger to them.* Assigning danger to a feeling or feelings means believing things will never get better and will only grow worse. Another way we assign danger to a feeling is believing that our feelings don't matter and no one wants to hear them. Adjusting how we view our emotions as either temporary, important, or normal reduces the pressure to have it all figured out and can relieve the intensity of our emotions. Try saying this mantra to yourself anytime things start to feel overwhelming or hopeless. If it doesn't resonate with you, think of another saying you can use to help yourself when your feelings become intense.

The Teen Years Are Tumultuous for Everyone

The teenage years are a critical part of development in the grand scheme of your life. It is a time when you are piecing together your identity—who you are, what you like, and how you manage life's many choices and options. When a person is trying to figure out what they do and don't want for their lives, emotions can be all over the place and lead to confusion. Your family may try to give you space or attempt to control parts of your life because they're watching you grow and change. They may try to protect you from real life and keep you in the dark, or they may expose you to the realities of adulthood. It's a time to recognize what you want and to go after it. Because you are challenging everything and feeling a lot of feelings at once, you will make a lot of mistakes, and your family (or other people you trust) will have to walk that path with you. Think of a safe person or people in your life who will help you understand what is happening, learn from your mistakes, and validate how challenging this time is.

A Blended Family Can Make Life Feel Even More Topsy-Turvy

While you're navigating your identity, your new family is figuring out theirs, too. Everyone's roles, needs, and expectations have changed. Becoming a blended family at a crucial time in your life will bring unexpected challenges that will require flexibility and the courage to keep talking and trying to learn from one another. As you progress through this workbook, you will find strategies to learn about yourself, communicate your feelings and needs with your family, and hopefully learn to adapt, which is a much-needed skill as you move into adulthood.

A MASSIVE TRANSITION
Unless others have been through it, they just won't get it. People will try to understand, but it takes someone who has personal experience to genuinely understand how big of a transition this actually is. Others may try to look for the positives, like celebrating every holiday and birthday twice, but the rest of the year can really get you down and change everything you believe and perceive about the world.

A LOSS OF FAMILY IDENTITY
What you knew to be your family has changed completely. A lot of pain comes with that realization and the need to fully grieve what has been lost. Grief can feel

painful and even permanent. I'll walk you through how to grieve in a healthy way so that you can be open to building a new family identity and feel stable again.

SHAME AND LOW SELF-WORTH

Have you ever thought that what you're going through might be your fault, or have you felt angry at your parents for not figuring out how to make their marriage work? Experiencing anger over what you've been through is an important part of the grieving process. Maybe you feel like everything in your life is fragile. Shame is the belief that we are bad and that we don't deserve the comfort, love, or security we truly seek. Everyone feels shame at different times in their lives. You don't need to change any of these feelings; rather, it's what you do with them that is important.

LONELINESS AND FEELING LIKE AN OUTSIDER IN YOUR HOME

When you are part of a blended family, it's common to feel like you're living in someone else's space and not your own. Maybe you feel like you don't have a place that is just yours where you can be yourself. Feeling like a lonely outsider is a familiar experience for many others who have gone through the same thing you're going through right now.

ANXIETY AND STRESS

Anxiety and stress are your body's emotional and physical responses to dealing with complicated and complex issues it hasn't dealt with before. Your body is constantly assessing every detail of your life to determine whether it is safe and develops automatic coping strategies that may be healthy or unhealthy. The exercises in this book can help you develop healthy long-term coping strategies.

Celebrate Your Strength

I want you to take a moment and look at all you are and all you've been through. Despite everything, you are still striving to move forward in a positive and healthy way. Maybe you feel strong and determined right now, or maybe you don't. Regardless of how you feel in this moment, I want you to speak to yourself words of confidence and love that acknowledge your strength.

Every day I'm getting up and trying again even when I don't feel like it.

I'm building my sense of self-love by acknowledging my feelings.

I believe I am strong and will adapt to the challenges I've already faced and the ones still yet to come.

You don't have to believe these words. The goal is to choose the thoughts that cross your mind. Choosing to feed yourself healthy thoughts will eventually become second nature. Just like the food you put in your body, your thoughts can either nourish or fatigue you. There will be up days when you feel like saying these affirmations, and there will be down days. Take it one day at a time.

No Matter What Your Family Looks Like, You Are Worthy of Love and Compassion

What is love and compassion? I believe having love and compassion is the ability to care about yourself or another person in a way that acknowledges their (or your) needs as a priority and seeking to understand them (or yourself) with fresh and open eyes. Every day we are evolving, growing, and changing. Everyone around us, whether we know it or not, is struggling. When we allow ourselves to feel certain emotions and make mistakes, it gives us more empathy for ourselves. If you see someone being super critical and judgmental of others, it's a good sign they can't practice love and compassion toward themselves, either. Throughout this journey you will feel a vast range of emotions—from being lost and hopeless to having clarity and hope for the future. No matter what you feel, go through, mess up, or challenge, you are worthy of love and compassion. You deserve to have the human experience of grief, the permission to change, and the ability to see yourself in a new way. Your new family may look very different compared to what your family once looked like. Some people will judge. Maybe you have judged the differences you see because you're worried what others may think. I assure you that no matter what your family looks like, just as you are worthy of love, so are they.

This Book Will Give You Tools to Heal and Cope with Change

I want to be here for you in the pages of this book. My hope is that the message you absorb while reading and using this workbook will stay with you throughout your life. This short time will teach you much about what lies ahead. You will see how much you are truly capable of. You will see that your emotions can teach you about what your needs are and how to communicate them. Together we will walk through the challenges ahead, and I'll be with you the whole way offering practical tools and insights into who you are. I have often found that as we go through our own challenges, we develop a sense of grace and empathy for the challenges, choices, and messes that others go through. I hope that when you are finished here you will see that life is messy and our growth lies in making choices rather than remaining stuck waiting for a perfect answer. I'll walk you through different therapy modalities that I often incorporate into my practice and personal life, and I will show you the tools I wish I had when I was going through exactly what you're experiencing right now—the blending of your new family.

Helping Yourself Will Help Your Blended Family in the Long Run

What you do for yourself will always have a direct impact on those around you. You often cannot change how others react or respond to you. However, when you change how you respond and react to those around you, it changes how people perceive you and often how they will interact with you in the future. You are influential, and what you do now can have a very positive impact on how your family heals and works together to build something special. For example, recognizing and owning your own feelings will help you better communicate them to your family. The better you understand and can communicate with your family, the more you'll get to know and support one another. This builds a new dynamic that helps others feel they can do the same. This may help decrease arguing and increase connection at home. That said, you are not responsible for how your family moves through life entirely. But you can have a special kind of power to positively influence how people see and treat you in the long run, which can deepen your relationships with others and yourself.

Let's Get Started

Be patient and give yourself time as you go through this workbook. You may find yourself going through it quickly, taking your time, or feeling resistance to even getting started. I believe that the information you need will present itself to you at the time you need it. Whatever way you choose to approach this book, and when, is completely up to you. I hope it will be a guide for you to notice without judgment what is coming up for you. The tools contained in this book are meant to be what you need them to be. In other words, take from them what you want. Take the tools that work for you, and leave behind what doesn't feel relevant or essential. You may find that you take one very specific tool from this book that stays with you for a lifetime. My ultimate hope is that this workbook is a resource for you to keep coming back to when you need it and that you learn to connect with yourself and others in a new way. Please know that you are not alone while you're working through this family transition. There are so many others in your same situation looking for the same answers. Together we will figure out where to go from here and learn to love ourselves better. Let's get started!

PART II

Your Blended Family Tool Kit

In part I, we focused on how challenging it can be to be part of a blended family. It's time to take you through your own experience of being in a blended family, to help you notice, reflect, and make some changes to what is happening within you and around you. We will walk through a variety of exercises and prompts that focus on noticing how our emotions play a role in our behavior. I'll teach you several ways to notice those emotions, calm or regulate those big feelings, and change the way you think about what is happening to you so you can respond in a way that gets your needs met and your voice heard. I'll take you through prompts that give you time to focus on what is happening both inside you and around you. Let's get started!

CHAPTER 1

Tune into You

This chapter is all about taking time to focus on and notice what is happening inside of you. We're looking for awareness here, not judgment of ourselves. We can't do any better until we know better. Remember that you've been through a lot and it takes time to adapt to change and learn your new life and how you want to show up in it. Spend time reflecting in this chapter on all that has been going on, believing that throughout the rest of this book you will be learning new tools and strategies to help you navigate this transition in a calm and effective way.

Casey's Story

Casey's mom has gotten remarried for the second time, and Casey doesn't get to see her dad as much because of his work schedule. She often feels lonely because her mom has to focus on other things right now, and it's not just the two of them anymore. It hasn't been in a while. She was really hopeful that after her mom's last breakup they would get to spend more time together. Casey noticed that she felt angry and frustrated. It didn't take much for her to lash out and slam the door to her room. With the help of a therapist and her mom, she was able to recognize that she was depressed because of all the changes in her life and learned that what she really wanted and needed was more one-on-one time with her mom. Casey began tracing her anger back to how connected she felt to her mom. If it was a busy week and there wasn't much time to spend together, Casey learned that she could identify her anger as a need for closeness, communicate her needs, and her mom would respond by making plans for them to be together without distractions.

Use Your Breathing to Notice Your Emotions

One of my favorite exercises to teach clients and use myself is called diaphragmatic breathing. Noticing and focusing your breathing can help you slow down racing thoughts and overwhelming emotions no matter where you are and who you're with. When you slow and focus your breathing, it regulates your heart rate and helps you direct your emotions instead of just reacting to everything you're feeling. Whether you're at school, in your room, or out with friends, try this breathing exercise:

1. Breathe in.

2. Move your breath slowly up and down while pushing your belly out.

3. Then pull your belly in as you breathe out.

It also helps to count the beats in your head as you breathe in and out. I prefer to count to four in my mind as I'm taking a deep breath in and pushing my belly out and counting to four again as I push my breath out of my mouth and pull my belly in. Give it a try right now and repeat it four times. Next time you notice that sneaky feeling of overwhelm, try this exercise out for better clarity and focus.

Relax Your Muscles

We can hold a lot of tension and stress in our bodies. Over time we fail to notice that tension and become easily frustrated. The goal is to become aware of your body and to make choices to both hold tension in areas and send a release to that same area as you need it. This exercise is meant to help you become aware of where you hold tension in your body and how to control the relaxation. To do this exercise, lie down on your bed or couch, or sit in a comfy chair.

1. Scrunch your toes as tight as you can, and then release.

2. Flex your toes up toward your knees, and then point your toes away from you, which will tense and release your calf muscles.

3. Tense up your rear as tight as you can, and then release.

4. Suck your belly in as tight as you can, and then release.

5. Grip your fingers as tight as you can, and then release.

6. Tighten your biceps as much as you can, and then release.

7. Pull your shoulders up toward your ears, and then release.

8. Close your eyes as tight as you can, and then open them.

9. Finally, move your head from side to side to elongate the sides of your neck, and then release.

Once you begin practicing this often, you will notice when your muscles become tense and recognize it as a signal that you need to bring relaxation to that part of your body.

Learn Yourself

Learning to check in with yourself is an important tool for understanding why you do what you do, based often on how you feel and the experiences that are happening to and around you. Below is a chart that you can fill in over a weeklong period. Each day you can check in by writing about an event that happened, the emotion you experienced during or after the event, and how you responded to that event. As you spend time tracking how certain events impact your mood and behavior, you can make more conscious choices about how you want to react and get a better idea of what emotions shape your decision-making.

EVENT	EMOTION	REACTION
was asked to do the dishes	*frustrated, tired*	*yelled and complained that I'm always doing everything*

The practice of checking in with yourself is important because in order to address a problem or symptoms, we have to first become aware of it. Change requires awareness. You may find that after doing this for a week you can begin to see trends in your behavior that will help you understand what your needs may be, which you can discuss with your family.

What Worked for You?

In the first three exercises, you've learned how to check in with yourself, slow and control your breathing, and become aware of tension you hold in your body. What exercise was the most impactful in terms of bringing about self-awareness? What did you learn about the emotions that are often present for you, how they impact your body, and the reactions they cause? Think about the exercise that was the most helpful for you and how you could continue using it in the future.

_____

_____

_____

_____

_____

_____

_____

_____

_____

_____

_____

_____

_____

_____

_____

_____

_____

Creating Mantras

It can be helpful to come up with a set way to check in with yourself when emotions get high. You won't always be able to predict when you will feel overwhelmed and need to use the skills you're learning in this workbook. (Oftentimes when we are overwhelmed, we won't use any of the skills because our brains are just trying to keep us safe and secure.) Practice being gentle with yourself when you mess up by creating a mantra like, *I'm trying my best even when I make mistakes*. Creating a mantra is a simple way to redirect your brain during an emotional event or after you realize you've made a mistake. Mantras are lifesavers for me because life is messy, and even with the best intentions, I don't always make the best choices when I'm upset or sad. The goal is not to be perfect but to show yourself grace and get back up and try again.

Exploring Primary and Secondary Emotions

It can often be hard to label a certain emotion right away. Start with some of the more predominant emotions like angry, sad, tired, or frustrated. These emotions are often what are referred to as *secondary emotions*—emotions that are easier to label but give very little information about what a person is really going through. *Primary emotions* are often hurt, grieving, lonely, vulnerable, or embarrassed. You can start by asking yourself, *If I feel angry, what might be going on that is causing the anger to want to protect me?* Anger and frustration are emotions that try to protect us from feeling lonely or not good enough. We will explore this in more depth in chapter 2.

Behavior Has a Big Impact on Our Emotions

Have you ever felt less motivation when you haven't moved your body in a while, or noticed feeling sad for longer when you listen to sad music? What you do has a direct impact on your overall mood. We get into vicious cycles of behavior that keep our mood exactly where it is: depressed, sad, overwhelmed, or easily frustrated.

For the next three days, use the provided grid to keep a log of your activities throughout the day and how you felt during or after doing those activities. For example, if you find yourself staying in bed, watching a lot of TV, and not responding to your friends' text messages, did you feel lonely or connected? In the next exercise, we will evaluate the activities that increased your mood to "positive" emotions and the activities that put you in a more negative headspace.

To be clear, all emotions are healthy, but many of us get stuck in emotional spaces that we can't seem to get out of. This exercise is all about finding out what you do that makes you feel the way you'd like to really feel.

	DAY #1	DAY #2	DAY #3
7 a.m.			
8 a.m.			
9 a.m.			
10 a.m.			
11 a.m.			

	DAY #1	DAY #2	DAY #3
12 p.m.			
1 p.m.			
2 p.m.			
3 p.m.			
4 p.m.			
5 p.m.			
6 p.m.			
7 p.m.			
8 p.m.			
9 p.m.			

Evaluating and Changing What We Do to Feel the Way We Want to Feel

Based on the tracking you did over the last week in the "Behavior Has a Big Impact on Our Emotions" exercise (page 20), we are going to evaluate what you were doing and who you were with when you felt the way you wanted to feel. You are starting to get to know yourself through these exercises. It takes more than a few days to get a good idea of what you really need, but when you write things down, you're more likely to go back to it and use it when you need it. Writing things down will also empower you when you're feeling down and struggling to find the motivation you need.

You will analyze the grid from the previous exercise and transfer the activities to the two columns based on how they made you feel. Now that you know what makes you feel better, you can come back to this exercise when you need that extra nudge to get up and get going. You can also remind yourself of some of the activities that don't always make you feel good so that you get really clear on making decisions that are in alignment with your goal of managing your emotions.

HAPPY ACTIVITIES	DEPRESSING ACTIVITIES

Talk to Yourself Like You Would a Friend

Changing the way we think about ourselves and our emotions ultimately impacts how we react to certain emotions and events. Let's explore some of the thoughts we have about ourselves and then evaluate what we truly want to believe and see in ourselves. As you move through this activity, think about what you would say to a friend who was saying something unhealthy or predominately negative to themselves. We are often kinder to others than we are to ourselves.

In this exercise, think of and write down some negative thoughts you had about yourself recently. On the right, write down an alternative thought that focuses more on your positive aspects. Here, I'll give you a couple of examples.

NEGATIVE THOUGHT	POSITIVE THOUGHT
I can't seem to do anything right.	*I know I keep trying.*
No one really cares about me.	*I can reach out if I need help.*

Checkpoint!

It can be difficult to process this much information about your feelings, thoughts, and reactions to life's experiences. As you think back on the last three exercises, what did you notice about your initial reactions? Did you notice any resistance or hesitation to trying them out? Were you open to trying them out, and did you find yourself learning something new? Resistance is a normal part of life, and so is trying something new. Learn to identify resistance and your natural reactions to things without judgment. Remember, awareness must happen before change.

_____

_____

_____

_____

_____

_____

_____

_____

_____

_____

_____

_____

_____

_____

_____

_____

_____

Getting Our Goals Together

You are at the very beginning of this workbook and learning all about yourself. It's an exciting time, but perhaps you are sensing some resistance to doing this work, or perhaps you're wondering if you can really fit this in among your other commitments and responsibilities.

In this exercise, I want you to take some time to explore what your goals are for this workbook. Think of a goal as something you would like to accomplish or get out of your efforts. Even if you are unsure, it's okay to explore the idea of using this as a check-in or to please the adult that bought the book for you. Be honest with yourself about what you need to gain from this experience, and do so without judgment toward yourself. Healthy, attainable goals are clear and manageable; you should be able to identify how often something will happen and when it will happen.

Next I want you to focus on realistically how much time you can dedicate to this workbook. Set goals that do not overwhelm you, and if you happen to do more, great. If you do the minimum of what you set out to do, that is great as well.

Using the provided checklist, write down at least three clear goals.

☐ *I will try at least one exercise from each chapter in this workbook one time per week.*

☐ *I will read this workbook for five minutes, three times per week.*

☐ _____

☐ _____

☐ _____

☐ _____

☐ _____

☐ _____

☐ _____

☐ _____

Developing Pros and Cons for Our Decisions

We usually approach goals with the idea that we will complete them—only to have life take over and move us in a different direction. We all need a way to practice making healthy choices when we are in a calm state of mind and not when we are experiencing a crisis or overwhelm. For this exercise, write down one goal you are trying to achieve. In the grid on the following page, you will see there is a space for describing the advantages and disadvantages of your goal based on your state of mind. Write down how working toward this goal will impact you when you are calm and regulating your emotions well. Then write down how working toward this goal could impact you when you are not in a good state of mind. This will help you prepare yourself for the inevitable changes that will come up while pursuing any goal.

Example Goal: I will practice deep breathing for five minutes a day.

	ADVANTAGE	DISADVANTAGE
Calm state of mind	*Deep breathing will help me feel in control of my emotions.*	*I may have to step away from friends and find a quiet place.*
Stressed state of mind	*It will reduce my heart rate and help me relax.*	*I might get anxious that it won't work and be unable to focus.*

Goal:

_____

_____

	ADVANTAGE	DISADVANTAGE
Calm state of mind		
Stressed state of mind		

Creating Checkpoints

A periodic time of reflection to refocus our thoughts and get in touch with our body goes a long way toward staying on track with our goals. We will be focusing on building sustainable and attainable goals for the work we're doing in this book. First, though, we must build a practice of self-reflection either daily or weekly that helps us reconnect to our goals, the tools we're learning, and our emotional state. Think about a day or time of day when you can have some consistency for a routine check-in with yourself in the future. I like combining this with an activity I always do, such as getting ready for work in the morning, walking to school, or Sunday night when I'm usually feeling some anxiety for the week ahead. If it helps you, too, think about an activity that you're always doing and use it as a time to check in with yourself.

Learning to Be Present

Take a few minutes to enjoy some fresh air through an open window, sitting outside, or going for a walk. When we engage in so much processing, we need to create room to just breathe and relax. Our brains can feel like they never stop, and then we don't know what to do with all the information we're taking in. If you're into doodling or writing, go ahead and use the space on this page to draw or write what you're seeing or noticing about the world around you. Ground yourself in the experience you're in by noticing small details, sounds, or smells you're picking up from wherever you are. Try to disconnect yourself from your head and from the moment by stopping and redirecting your focus to the details of what is happening all around you. Focus on colors, sounds, tastes, and smells that appeal to you, and describe them in your mind.

Learn to Love Journaling

Journaling is a rewarding hobby that lets you reflect on your life and gives you space to open up to yourself. There won't always be someone there to listen to you share your thoughts. A big part of developing a healthy relationship with yourself is spending time getting to know your own thoughts and the wisdom you have to share with yourself. Journaling is a tool you can use when you want to process something that you don't yet want to share with others or there is no one to share with. There is no right or wrong way to journal. Some people draw sketches of what they are thinking in their journal. Others will pour out their hearts and write freely without analyzing their thoughts. In this exercise, try to write your first journal entry. I want you to write whatever is in your head without any expectation or judgment. It can be one sentence, a whole page, or a paragraph. There are no limits, and this is only for your eyes.

_____

_____

_____

_____

_____

_____

_____

_____

_____

_____

_____

_____

_____

Embracing Uncertainty

As you have been thinking about your goals for this book and what you might get out of it, did you notice any uncertainty? Sometimes we approach a goal with little clarity about what we might get from it. Embracing uncertainty willingly and openly is a great skill to learn and take with you into adulthood. How do you deal with uncertainty? What could be possible for you if you responded to uncertainty in a different way?

_____

_____

_____

_____

_____

_____

_____

_____

_____

_____

_____

_____

_____

_____

_____

_____

Finding Who and What Brings Us Comfort

Having a practice that you regularly turn to when life feels chaotic, messy, or unclear is beneficial for maintaining your mental health. During times of anxiety or turbulence, we need things and people we can count on to give us a sense of stability and safety.

In this practice, I want you to identify a person who means a lot to you, who you can or have built a relationship with, and who can be there to support you when you need it most. Sometimes you will need an outlet to vent, and other times you might want to have fun with someone without thinking about all the things going on in your life. When you name this person, think about how you can build a practice of engaging with them more regularly for both support and connection.

Next reach out to them via text and set something up. It could be a time to just chat or a plan to go somewhere. If you feel a little nervous about this, ask your person how they are doing and try to get a read on what they need in a friendship or relationship as well. Being a good friend involves giving someone what they need and also getting your needs met in the relationship. It's all about creating balance for both people involved. Use the lines below to brainstorm the people you might reach out to and what you could suggest doing together.

_____

_____

_____

_____

_____

_____

_____

_____

_____

Jason's Story

Jason had to move because of his parents' divorce. Not only was he moving to a new town, but he was also leaving behind all his old friends and had to attend a new school. He felt angry and resentful about the divorce and all the change in his life. He was not sure he could or wanted to make new friends, and he definitely felt like his mom was more involved in her new relationship than in his life. That anger started to grow, and pretty soon he was isolating himself from everyone because he felt everyone let him down. A few weeks after starting at his new school he met some potential new friends. He identified one guy he felt he could grow a deeper friendship with. He put himself out there and started reaching out over text and setting up times to hang out after school. As he began spending time with this friend, he noticed the anger starting to go away, and he began to see that some people could be trusted. Happiness and connection were becoming possible again, and before he knew it, he found himself feeling more at home and able to make an effort at building a relationship with his soon-to-be stepdad.

WRAP-UP

You have already worked through quite a few tools for learning how both your reactions to things and your feelings impact one another. We have put together some goals for the work we will be doing in this book, acknowledging that resistance is always a part of the growing process and you won't always make decisions with a lot of clarity. The goal is to have forward motion and keep putting one foot in front of the other. In the next chapter, we'll do a deeper dive into your feelings, where they are coming from, and what you can do with them.

CHAPTER 2

Examine Your Feelings

Feelings are rarely logical. They can come out of nowhere, stay for a bit, or sometimes stay for a really long time. Many people struggle with identifying their emotions and often react to those emotions in ways that are not in alignment with what they truly want or need from a given situation. Labeling our emotions takes a great deal of time and energy but will bring us closer to ourselves. One thing to remember is that feelings don't always have to have reason behind them to be valid. Life is hard, and the stage of life that you are currently in will present unique challenges. On top of that, you are living in a blended family situation that comes with its own set of circumstances and other peoples' personalities and needs that can overshadow your own. What you will learn in this chapter is that every emotion is valid, deserves to be seen, and has a need behind it.

Aaliyah's Story

Aaliyah felt sad for no reason most of the time. After her dad started dating someone new, she felt the need to pull further and further away from people. The things she used to enjoy didn't interest her anymore, and she didn't want to talk about herself to anyone. She often felt misunderstood and lonely, yet her desire to be alone was stronger than her desire to really connect with anyone else. She began writing in her journal and noticing that behind all the sadness was a grief that her relationship with her dad had changed. He was her rock and best friend. They used to do everything together, and now they barely hang out. With the help of a therapist, Aaliyah was able to recognize that she was depressed and needed to explore with her dad how their relationship had changed. They began going to therapy sessions together and spending more time together again. Aaliyah noticed that she wasn't as sad anymore, and when she did begin feeling sad again, she knew it was because she needed more connection and learned how to ask for it.

Learn Your Emotions

We think it should be easy to just come up with a word for whatever it is we are feeling. However, that is usually not the case. Usually we grow up without really learning how to label our emotions, much less get in touch with them, manage them, and prevent them from interfering with our actions. One of my favorite things to have on hand in my office for clients is an emotion vocabulary. For this exercise, do an online search for "emotion vocabulary." Take a look at the different lists available to you and pick one that resonates with you. Either take a picture of it on your phone or print it out to have on hand; use it to check in with yourself before journaling or expressing your emotions to someone. You may be surprised by which emotions jump out at you. If there are some emotions you don't recognize, I encourage you to look up the definition of those emotions online. Studying your feelings and learning what different emotions look like will help you become more adept at identifying which ones you're experiencing and subsequently understand what you may need.

Making Emotions More Real

Think of an emotion you may be feeling right now or have felt recently. You can also use the emotional vocabulary chart you saved from the "Learn Your Emotions" exercise (page 36). Now that you know the labels for a variety of emotions, choose one to bring to life. Write down the emotion first, and then think of it as you would a character in a story. You started by giving that emotion a name. Next you are going to give it a personality. Write out a character sketch of that emotion. Think about when that emotion usually comes up and what that emotion might make you think or say. Think about how you notice that emotion in your body and how it makes you behave. I love this exercise because every emotion we experience is a part of us. By bringing our emotions to life in this way, we become more familiar with them and better able to listen to what they are trying to communicate to us. An example might be the following:

Sad

When I feel sad, I can tell she is losing energy. She has been drained by having to talk to people all the time. Sad wants to spend time alone in her room and watch TV to distract from how difficult life feels sometimes. Sad wants to eat chocolate and wear comfy clothes.

Learning to Just Notice

We are usually our own worst critic when it comes to our feelings, behaviors, and body. We cannot make any changes to our lives of long-term value or sustainability if we start from a place of judgment. I want you to use this exercise to learn to *just notice* what is happening in your mind by labeling emotions from a nonjudgmental place. Starting right now, I'd like you to get in the habit of saying, *I'm noticing that I am feeling sad* or *I'm noticing that I'm feeling angry and wanting to yell or break something*. Labeling an emotion without judgment helps reduce the intensity of that emotion in your body. You can use this "just noticing" technique when you are feeling hypercritical of yourself or when you find it difficult to understand your actions. Take this one step further and find a mirror. Look at yourself and say anything you need to say or have been afraid to say. You can even take a selfie and write *I'm noticing I'm amazing*. Be creative and use this technique to remind yourself of your humanity. Your feelings matter and are important!

Write It Down!

When we write something down, we are more likely to follow through on it. Get out some strips of paper or note cards, and write down affirmations or practices you can do whenever you need a pick-me-up. For example:

I'm doing the best I can right now.

I'm allowed to make mistakes and learn from them.

I have the ability to calm myself through deep breathing whenever I need to.

I can feel whatever emotion comes up for me.

   I love doing this and picking one at random to try on a whim. It brings spontaneity into your mindfulness practice and helps you switch things up a bit if a certain practice or exercise is feeling boring. You can even search online for mindfulness exercises or affirmations to add more variety to this practice and utilize these cards or prompts to help you build a lifestyle of mindfulness and connection to your body.

Be Curious About Your Emotions

We all have a range of emotions that feel acceptable, and any emotions outside of that range are ones we don't give ourselves permission to feel. Some of us have bigger ranges where we are really allowed to freely express ourselves, and others of us can't or don't feel like we are allowed to express ourselves. What has been your experience with emotional expression? Think about what you may need in order to feel free to express yourself without being judged or shut down by others or yourself.

_____

_____

_____

_____

_____

_____

_____

_____

_____

_____

_____

_____

_____

_____

_____

_____

_____

Learning to Look Underneath the Surface

All of us experience certain emotions that seem to come to the surface more than others. I call these protective emotions. They protect us or benefit us in some way from vulnerability or being hurt by others. These emotions are usually anger, frustration, sadness, exhaustion, and overwhelm. These commonly used and felt emotions are valid. However, as we learned in the previous chapter, they don't fully give voice to the emotions they are protecting. Those more vulnerable or quiet emotions go unsaid or unnoticed, and it's harder to identify the needs behind those emotions. In the table below, write down some of the emotions you may usually experience, and then next to them identify what emotions might be below the surface.

I FEEL . . .	WHAT'S UNDERNEATH . . .
angry all the time	*is loneliness and fear of not being wanted*

There is no right or wrong way to do this, but checking in with your own intuition can help you tap into what's underneath your feelings of anger, frustration, sadness, fatigue, and overwhelm.

Self-Acceptance

The relationship you have with yourself will set the tone for every other relationship you develop in your life. When you learn to love and accept yourself, the need for others' opinions and validation will change for you. We are going to learn a meditation practice that will help you become fiercely loyal to yourself, in any form, and be present with any emotion that comes up.

1. Start by setting up a clear and comfortable place in your bedroom or wherever you feel safe.

2. Set a timer on your phone for one minute, and let yourself feel whatever you feel without judgment or attempts to change or control your thoughts. If there is a difficult feeling or thought you're avoiding, allow yourself to feel it for this one minute.

3. When the timer goes off, try to put the difficult feeling or thought back away in its box and do a distracting activity like listening to music, watching a TV show, or reading a book.

You can practice this exercise daily before you watch TV or do any other distracting activity. The goal here is to teach your body that all your emotions are healthy and can be felt. Stick with manageable times, like one minute, and then move on to a distracting activity.

Music That Tames Our Minds

We all need music and creative expression in our lives to get us out of our heads and help us feel less lonely. Take a moment to think about what song you listen to, book you read, or show you watch that makes you feel a little less alone in this world. You get to choose whatever it is that works for you and use this creative outlet anytime you get in your feelings. You can use this activity in conjunction with the "Self-Acceptance" exercise (page 41). After the timer goes off and you're finished feeling your feelings, you can use this creative outlet to move your thoughts and distract yourself to a place in your mind that feels good for you.

Who Do You Admire?

Who is a person in your life that you admire? This person can be in your day-to-day life, like a parent, teacher, or friend, or this person can also be a celebrity or public figure. Think about why this is someone you admire and describe their qualities you would like to see in yourself. When you find yourself in a funk, ask yourself what this person might do.

_____

_____

_____

_____

_____

_____

_____

_____

_____

_____

_____

_____

Loyalty to Self

Now let's combine three exercises from this chapter: "Learning to Just Notice" (page 38), "Learning to Look Underneath the Surface" (page 40), and "Self-Acceptance" (page 41). Think about how you can insert these quick exercises into your day-to-day life. Maybe you can plan to practice these exercises on the bus ride home from school or Sunday evenings when you're starting to get anxious about going back to school the next day. Maybe it can be Friday afternoons when you know you will be home for the whole weekend with your new family. Think about the times in your life that you may need the exercises the most to help you through the hard times that never seem to stop coming.

Distracting Activities

We can't feel our emotions all the time. That gets way too overwhelming and, quite frankly, unpleasant. Many people do everything they can to numb their emotions because they fear the feelings might never go away. I want to encourage you to accept your emotions and learn when it might help you to move away from them in a healthy way. Use the lines provided to come up with a list of five distracting activities you can do when your emotions are causing you to feel overwhelmed. Your brain has to become completely distracted in order to move away from certain emotions. For example, you can listen to a podcast, really concentrate on the lyrics to a song that is opposite of your mood, or count the number of people in a room you are in. When you've chosen five distracting things, write down the details of each specific distraction. That way you don't even have to think about how to implement them when you're overwhelmed.

☐ _____

☐ _____

☐ _____

☐ _____

☐ _____

Detecting an Emotional Crisis

When it comes to working with our emotions, we are all going to hit a point when we won't want to use the tools we are learning, and we won't want to change. When that happens, it's because the intensity of the emotion you are feeling has put your body into flight, fight, or freeze mode. That is when an emotion or experience has communicated to your body that it is time to do whatever is necessary to keep you emotionally or physically safe. For some people, they fight and rage and won't let a subject go. Others will withdraw and not want to talk about it. Some people will sit and not move or react to what is happening around them. These reactions happen to everyone. Not only can you not control it, but you can't always detect when it is going to get to this point.

Once you notice that this has happened or is happening, you will want to try to engage in one of your activities from the "Distracting Activities" exercise (page 43). Next, when you are finally calm, which usually takes about 20 to 30 minutes of distraction, ask yourself, *What happened right before I noticed that overwhelming emotion?* Asking yourself questions after a fight, flight, or freeze situation activates the part of the brain that helps you regulate your emotions. You can also come up with your own questions you'd like to ask yourself and write them on the lines provided.

_____

_____

_____

_____

_____

_____

_____

_____

_____

_____

Resting Pose

Let's take a little break from writing and thinking, and practice a meditation and breathing exercise.

1. Find somewhere comfy where you can lie flat on your back. Lie down and imagine every part of your body from your feet to your head melting into the floor or bed.

2. Extend your arms out from your body, close your eyes, and establish your natural breathing rhythm.

3. Track the gentle in breath and out breath. You do not have to try to control your breathing, just notice it and follow it with your mind.

This is a fantastic way to slow your body, regulate your emotions, and turn down your mind. Not only are you doing something with your body, but you are also connecting it with your mind by noticing your breathing and being conscious of your body on the flat space. I recommend trying this nightly as you are getting ready for bed, as a commitment to yourself to reduce stress, increase awareness of your body, and regulate your emotions.

Compassion Practice

Talk to yourself like you talk to a friend. Many of us have heard that phrase because we are often harder on ourselves than we are on others. When you have been experiencing a hard week or you find it difficult or unmotivating to practice the things you are learning, think about what advice or empathy you would give to a friend and how you might encourage them to try again. You can use this practice whenever you feel stuck in your feelings or lack motivation to act. We don't need more people telling us all we are not doing; we are hard enough on ourselves. Focus on giving yourself what you truly need, which is unconditional love, empathy, and guidance for moving forward.

Connecting with the Day

Think about your favorite time of day. Mine is the morning. I love waking up before everyone else, sitting outside, noticing the sunrise, listening to the birds, and thinking about how grateful I am for the new day. I want you to think about your favorite time of day and what you love about it. As you are thinking about that, plan for some time either today or tomorrow, at your favorite time of day, to either open a window, sit outside, or go for a walk. This is your time that you are creating just for yourself. You can have your favorite drink with you and take in the day. Notice the parts of the day you love the most, and recognize them in that moment. Take in your surroundings using any of your five senses of touch, taste, smell, sound, and/or vision. Notice those things and tell them to yourself in your mind. For example, *I can see the beautiful sunset with its colors of orange and red* or *I can smell the salt in the air.*

Mind-Body Connection

There are many different poses you can hold with your body that teach you to be mindful of the sensations you experience. They can bring your full mind into awareness of where you are at, what you are feeling, and help you breathe into that. If you haven't already, try searching online for yoga poses or breathing techniques that you may like to try at home. Even better if you want to connect with a local gym, YMCA, or community recreation center that offers yoga classes. Yoga is a wonderful form of movement that enhances a mind-body connection. Regulating your emotions is heavily reliant on bringing your mind into full awareness of what is happening in your body and learning how you can control the tension in certain places of your body using your breath. When you learn where some places hold tension, you can also begin to ask yourself questions about what feelings you may be experiencing or holding in those parts of your body.

Learning the Mind-Body Connection

For many of us, it can take a long time to understand how our mind and body connect based on our emotions. What is your experience with your family and friends when it comes to learning about emotions, expressing them, and regulating them? Think about what you have been taught, what you currently believe, and how what you are learning is changing your awareness.

Becoming Your Own Best Friend

As you reflect on some nice things you would tell a friend, did you notice a difference between your thoughts for someone else versus the thoughts you have about yourself? We are often much kinder to others than we are to ourselves. Think about a situation you're struggling with right now, and write down what you really want to hear a friend say to you. Now offer those kind words to yourself as encouragement.

Jaxon's Story

Jaxon never remembered a time when his parents lived in the same house. He grew up knowing that one week he would be with one parent and another week with the other parent. There was a routine and rhythm to how life went, and he never expected it to change—until one parent decided to get married. He knew his new stepparent and their kids but had never thought about having to learn to live with a bigger family with different cultural traditions. At first, he didn't really notice the change, but over time he noticed himself becoming easily frustrated and would yell at his family for seemingly no reason. There were more people to navigate, and home became loud and boisterous. The cooking smells were all different from what he was accustomed to, and the meals were delicious but unfamiliar. He began trying to become more aware of what happened right before he would lash out and used the help of emotional vocabulary to notice that he was feeling anxious about the change that was happening and the possibility of new changes that he couldn't foresee. Now that he knew he was anxious, he began listening to music that made him feel more relaxed and podcasts about how to manage anxiety and change. He used the practices he learned from those podcasts, such as breathing strategies and affirmations, to slowly regulate his emotions and learn to accept that change was a part of life that didn't have to be scary.

EXAMINE YOUR FEELINGS

49

WRAP-UP

Examining your feelings is the best way to get to know yourself and identify your needs, and prepares you for sharing those feelings and needs with others. Our emotions can feel so conflicting and confusing sometimes, and that is okay. You may feel two very different emotions about the same issue. For example, you may feel guilty and relieved about something because you made a choice that felt right for you even if it made another person mad. It is completely normal to have emotions that don't make sense. My motto is, you've got to name the emotion in order to understand what to do with it. Take all the time you need to practice labeling your emotions, ask for help when needed, or use an emotional vocabulary list. This is a lifelong journey, and your emotions and their intensities will change. Remember that a feeling will come and a feeling will go. These things you're feeling right now won't last forever.

CHAPTER 3

Prioritize Self-Care

Living in a blended family situation with new personalities and people in the house can leave you feeling many emotions, including feelings of loss, loneliness, abandonment, or comparison. In order to give your best to support others and deal with challenging emotions and situations, you have to take care of yourself first. In this chapter, we will review what self-care is and how to build strategies that help you focus on self-compassion, self-love, and embracing who you are. We will be working with different forms of self-care and building lifestyle habits that will help you tackle all the challenges you currently face and prepare you for the challenges ahead.

Tina's Story

Tina grew up in a Black family living in a predominantly Black community. Her parents divorced when she was little, and all she knew was the love of both her parents when she was with them. As she got older, both her parents remarried and one relocated. One married a white partner with children in a predominantly white community, and one remarried and stayed in the same community. When Tina was with one parent, she was the only Black child in a house full of white kids. Tina felt isolated. With the other parent, she had the house all to herself in a familiar neighborhood. As she grew up, she didn't know where she fit into the dynamic of her bigger family and how to put all the pieces together to make sense of who she was, what her family was "supposed" to look like, and how to adapt in friend groups. She took up creative writing and filmmaking and found an outlet to examine who she really was and the passion that would drive her in her career today. Feeling supported by her parents to embark on this hobby with full force became her safe haven. Being able to help tell the stories of others is what truly made her feel most inspired.

What Does Self-Care Mean to You?

Self-care is different for everyone. You can't follow a certain trend or look at what makes someone else happy to know what is going to make you happy. Self-care is part of a self-exploration process. What works now may not work six months from now. Learning yourself will help you stay in alignment and prevent you from pushing yourself to keep doing something that doesn't feel like care. For this exercise, I want you to take some time to define what you think self-care means for you. For me, self-care means consistently engaging in activities that align with what I value (e.g., health, creative writing, and spending time with family). As my life has changed, my values have changed, and I have learned that I am allowed to change over time. If something doesn't feel right, it probably isn't anymore. Write your definition of self-care in the following box. Feel free to add a drawing of your definition, too.

Self-Care is . . .

What We Think about Ourselves Matters

The greatest and most important part of self-care is often overlooked: our thoughts! What we say and believe about ourselves matters. If I'm having a particularly crummy day and I want to ignore everyone because I believe no one would care anyway, that is definitely going to have an impact on my mood and the way I interact with others. If we want to change our reality and make an impact on our emotional well-being, we have to learn to be in control of what we think and believe. You get to decide what you want to believe about a given situation in order to determine how you go about handling it.

I want you to take a few minutes to brainstorm all the words you want to feel about yourself in the lines below. Then, come up with six affirmations based on these words and write them into the sticky notes on the next page. Creating these affirmations is an important step toward your self-care. Reciting these affirmations gives you an opportunity to redirect your thoughts and focus when you find yourself getting lost in big emotions and fears. When you write your affirmations about yourself, take a picture on your phone and make yourself look at these affirmations when you need a pick-me-up. You might even write them onto actual sticky notes and post them around your room. I'll write one of mine below to get you started.

Example: *I'm awesome, I know it, and others will know it, too.*

_____

_____

_____

_____

_____

_____

_____

_____

_____

Setting a Self-Care Structure

When we write something down, we are creating a plan, and we are more likely to make sure it happens. That is why I'm asking you to do so much writing in this book! It's one thing to talk about accomplishing things, but it's better to make intentional plans to incorporate the strategies you know are going to help you feel better and more connected. You've already defined what self-care is, and now I want you to think about starting small. If we try to change our whole self-care routine and add multiple exercises to our lives at once, it can be too much and we can easily get overwhelmed and quit. When you say yes to something, it also means you have to say no to something else to balance your time. For example, if I believe that self-care is exercising for one hour a day, that means I'll have to give up something that I typically do every day for one hour in order to make exercise happen. I want you to think about what is really important, how long and frequently you want to do it, and what you will have to say "no" to in order to make it happen.

Follow these steps to complete the table:

1. Think about all the things you are doing right now that aren't working for you, and write them in the column labeled "Not working."

2. Next, in the "Self-care" column, write down the things you would like to do on a daily basis for self-care that you will replace the things in the "Not working" column with.

3. Finally, in the last column labeled "Time and frequency," write down how much time you can realistically dedicate daily to your self-care activities by eliminating more things that aren't working for you.

You can revisit this exercise anytime you need if you feel like your self-care routine isn't working or needs to be changed up. Here's an example to get you started.

NOT WORKING	SELF-CARE	TIME AND FREQUENCY
watching TV for 3 hours after school	*go outside for a walk, run, or meditation*	*go out for a walk 3x per week after school and ask a friend to come with me*

NOT WORKING	SELF-CARE	TIME AND FREQUENCY

A Moment for Reflection

Take a moment to think about what your experience with self-care has been. When you defined self-care in the "What Does Self-Care Mean to You?" exercise (page 55), did you notice that what you once believed about self-care has changed? If so, how? Self-care is something we all do whether we know it or not. The first thing we have to do is notice how we might already be trying to care for ourselves, determine if those things are still helping, and decide if something needs to change.

_____

_____

_____

_____

_____

_____

_____

_____

_____

_____

_____

_____

_____

_____

_____

_____

_____

Redefining What We Do

Take a look at the way you already move through life. Maybe you get up every day, eat breakfast, take a shower, and head to school. Maybe you talk to friends, do your homework, and end the day with watching Netflix. There is a lot of self-care already happening in that day. By changing the meaning of all or some of those things to be self-care, we don't change the action at all but instead change our mindset—our body changes how it views the action, making it feel more like self-care instead of just something we do. Take a moment to write down the things you do every day. For example, you can use any of the activities I listed at the beginning of this paragraph. Now, next time you do any of those activities, I want you to think to yourself, *This is my form of self-care.*

_____

_____

_____

_____

_____

_____

_____

Moving Our Body to Change Our Minds

Did you know that you can change your feelings by moving your body in small ways? For example, when you straighten your spine and sit up tall, your body assumes you feel confident. If you are feeling tense or sad, you can move your shoulders up and down. It doesn't take much to change your whole perspective and outlook on things. Even try moving your head from side to side when you're feeling lonely and notice what you see around you. These small movements won't be noticed by anyone but you and communicate to your brain that something has changed and it can feel or see something differently.

Our Bodies Need to Move

Self-care is multifaceted. How we care for ourselves can embody how we think, how we move, who we spend time with, and how we spend time with ourselves. In this exercise, we're going to get out of the house and do an activity you've always wanted to try with a person you'd enjoy sharing it with. This is going to take some vulnerability, especially if asking people for help is hard or you fear rejection. Remember that everyone struggles with those fears, even if it doesn't seem like it.

Pick one activity you would love to try or an activity you used to love and would like to try again. Ask one of your favorite people, such as a parent, friend, or family member, to accompany you. When we move our bodies in a fun way with the intention of building self-care and self-love, it creates progress that supports us in creating more momentum toward our goals and needs. The goal here is to get moving by trying something new or returning to something we loved.

Learning to Let It Be

Get into the habit of telling yourself it's okay to change and to not always have an "on" day. We sometimes get stuck in this belief that we have to do everything perfectly without critically evaluating if the self-care we chose for today is going to work for us or not. You can have an "off" day and not be a failure. You can get back on track the next day. Give yourself grace by not always doing something the way you think it should be done. Checking in with yourself is vital to staying in touch with yourself and building self-love. Make a practice of asking yourself, *Is what I'm doing right now making me feel like I care and love myself?*

Do Nothing for a Bit

We have talked a lot about doing, and now I want you to focus on being. Just relaxing by yourself and doing nothing. You can do this for five minutes or several hours. Our bodies need to rest as much as they need to move. Boredom can be hard, and not being productive can make us feel anxious. Figure out a length of time to commit to this exercise, and make it a point to let your body be in a full state of rest. Depending on where you live, what surrounds you, and your family situation, you will need to get creative and maybe even have a conversation with a parent to communicate what you are doing so you do not get interrupted. I enjoy having something to look at when I'm letting my body rest, like a window or wall while lying on my bed. You get to choose what works best for you!

When you've completed this time of relaxation, reflect on the following questions and write your observations:

1. When I was resting, what emotions came up for me?

_____

_____

2. What was most restful about this experience?

_____

_____

3. What was difficult about this experience for me?

_____

_____

4. What might I need to change or incorporate into this time of rest to make it more meaningful and restful for me in the future?

_____

_____

Evaluate What Is Working

You've been trying some of these activities for a little bit. In this exercise, you will be self-assessing which aspects of your self-care routine seem to be helping and what things you are doing that may be causing you more stress or just not making you feel any different at all. I can't emphasize enough that you are allowed to change and it's okay if some things that you're trying out don't work for you. You are the driver and curator of your own life.

Once you recognize what isn't working for you, I want you to reevaluate and make changes to your routine. Track your new routine in this table. I'll start by giving you three examples from my own life that have helped me reevaluate the type of self-care I'm doing and will hopefully help you structure any changes to your routine.

Self-care shouldn't make us feel more stressed out. If you find that what you thought would work isn't working, you can always make changes.

WHAT I AM DOING	WHAT'S MY NEW PLAN?
Working out four times a week	Working out only two times a week on my days off
Journaling every evening before I go to bed	Journaling one weekend morning to reflect on the week as a whole
Ordering books online and reading them at home	Going to a bookstore and enjoying a coffee while I read a new book I've chosen

Lean into Your Intuition

How much do you trust the voice in your head? Do you find it difficult to listen to what your gut intuition says and worry it will steer you in the wrong direction? It can be difficult to build trust in what your gut intuition tells you. However, learning it and trusting in it will help you throughout the entirety of your life.

_____

_____

_____

_____

_____

_____

_____

_____

_____

_____

_____

_____

_____

_____

_____

_____

_____

_____

_____

Challenge Your Mind

We need to stay challenged when it comes to trying and learning new things. Self-care is always about learning, growing, developing, and nurturing ourselves. If we are not intentional about tackling new projects we have never tried before or pushing ourselves past our own comfort zones, we won't grow.

In this exercise, you are going to identify three new skills, projects, or hobbies you would like to learn and try at least once. Make a list of the three new things you're going to try and the anticipated completion dates to shoot for, then check the boxes as you complete your goals. Think about activities you have always wanted to try or learn. You are going to feel nervous and hopefully a little excited, but know that perfection isn't what you're aiming for; rather, it's to challenge yourself to try something outside of your comfort zone!

The best way to know you're choosing an ideal activity is by observing a slight sense of anxiety or worry about being able to complete them. Usually anxiety comes up in these situations *because* they are new and have never been tried. When you notice this anxiety, let it be your teacher for this exercise. I like to tell my clients that if you don't feel like throwing up just a little bit, you're probably not challenging yourself enough or striving for something that is really important to you.

☐ _____

☐ _____

☐ _____

Relax Your Mind

Two exercises back-to-back that have you doing two totally different things? Yes! Why? Because there is a thing in life called balance. Balance is the idea that we are checking in with ourselves and learning that with pushing forward, there is also a need to slow down and reflect on our progress, what we've learned, where we are going, and if we need to change course. Think of this as the necessary break during a marathon when you grab some water, catch your breath, and take care of your body's needs. In this exercise, you will be doing something that comes naturally to you. It doesn't require any pushing or much effort. It can be listening to music or baking your favorite cookies. This activity shouldn't require you to think hard, and it should allow you to be present in the moment. It's healthy and necessary to slow down and let things flow naturally for a minute as a reset to the grind of personal development. This can look different for everyone. Some love to go for an outdoor run. Others enjoy writing and recording music in the privacy of their bedroom. Whatever you choose to do, let it be easy and natural and void of comparison to others.

Finding and Choosing Our People

I believe we all need to feel a little less alone in the world. Self-care is something we do independently for ourselves, but we were never designed to go at it alone. Who we surround ourselves with will have a huge impact on our lives. If the people around us are motivated, driven, and working hard to learn and better themselves, then that will influence us in our decision-making and motivation. If the people around us are really sad and keep doing the same old things, then they will likely have a huge negative impact on our motivation and mood. You must critically evaluate who you spend time with, what you share with them, and think about how you feel when you are with them. What keeps you in those relationships, and do you fear loneliness if you step away from those friendships or relationships? Part of your development process may look like building a new friend group. When you try new hobbies and skills, you will meet new people. What I'm teaching you in this workbook may cause you to lose old relationships in order to grow and gain new, healthier relationships. Growth is painful but often necessary.

Do I Need Accountability?

Accountability is having someone who knows what you are trying to accomplish in your life and checks in with you periodically to make sure it's happening. That person will also encourage you to keep pushing forward when times get hard and remind you why you chose these goals.

Reflect on one person in your life that you trust and who can hold you accountable. This can be a therapist, parent, family member, friend, or teacher. The vulnerable thing I want you to do is set up a time to talk with this person. Take this workbook with you if you feel comfortable, and share your goals for this time in your life.

Finally, think specifically on the type of accountability you need or want. Do you want them to check in with you frequently? Do you want to just know that you can reach out to them for inspiration and motivation? Or do you want them to be the person you can vent to if something isn't going well and you know that they won't judge you? Play out the conversation in your head, and write it on the following lines in pencil. Do not overthink it on the first round. Come back to it at the end and make changes until you've got everything written down that you want to.

_____

_____

_____

_____

_____

_____

_____

_____

_____

_____

_____

Intention Setting

Every week I think about the three words I want to feel throughout each day. For example, I may want to feel rested, productive, and connected. Then I think about the way my week will be structured based on time and activities to ensure that those three values or feelings will be reflected in my schedule. You can write this in a journal, put it on a sticky note, or create a document for it on your phone to keep track. Some weeks you will get it right, and some weeks you won't. The goal is to learn how to be intentional in how you feel and live your life so that you don't feel like you're just surviving all the time.

How Have You Changed?

We have covered a lot about self-care, what it means to you, and how to build a plan to incorporate it into your life in a way this is intentional and thoughtful. As you reflect on what you have learned, what have you noticed about how your thoughts or behaviors have changed since starting this workbook? What has been your biggest takeaway so far about how you live your life and what you need or want to do with what you've learned?

_____

_____

_____

_____

_____

_____

_____

_____

_____

Gabby's Story

Gabby was a straight-A student who never slowed down for one minute. She found that the busier she was, the less she had to think about all the changes happening in her family, and the less she had to be at home. She constantly felt tired, irritable, and never really good enough. She kept pushing herself and keeping all her feelings to herself. In fact, she mostly tried to pretend everything was fine all the time. She didn't want to think about her life and her feelings because she felt helpless to change anything that was happening to her family. She recognized that she did need to slow down and learn her feelings, but she didn't know where to start and who to talk to. She noticed that other kids her age were talking to the school counselor and getting help. She went over her lunch period to talk with the school counselor and found out there were groups at the school for students to talk about what they were going through and get support. She also learned that if she needed to vent, the school counselor was just right down the hall, and it was okay to ask for help. She slowly started to open up to people she trusted, began trying new hobbies out at school, and helped others through tutoring. She started to feel like she had purpose, connection, and vulnerability.

WRAP-UP

Self-care is something that will evolve over time and does require checking in with yourself about where your life is and where you want it to be. Self-care is sometimes really challenging and at other times very easy and natural. Know that it is okay to ask for help and that you are not alone in the struggle to figure out what works for you and how to make it through tough circumstances like living in a blended family. As you begin to trust yourself and your intuition, you will find that practicing self-care will become more second nature to you. The good news is, you're learning this stuff early on in your life, which will have a profound impact on you when you eventually move away from your family and begin an independent life of your own.

CHAPTER 4

Embrace New Relationships

You didn't get much of a choice when it came to picking your new family, and the dynamics can turn your life upside down. All the new personalities and expectations can feel really overwhelming. Some of us keep our heads down, don't say much, and try to fly under the radar. Others feel like they have to please everyone and make all these relationships work from the start. No matter where you are in this process or what you may be feeling about the new people in your family, this chapter is designed to help you identify healthy expectations, reconnect after a difficult interaction, establish and communicate your boundaries, and build trust and nurture the relationships in your life.

Griffin's Story

Griffin never wanted life to change. He loved his family, and they pretty much did everything together. After his parents' divorce, Griffin often felt lost, confused, and sad about having to split everything up and all the family's traditions changing. Now that his parents are both remarried, he spends holidays with new people, doing things in a completely different way than what he wanted or remembered when growing up. He noticed that he was often disappointed and wanted to avoid the holidays altogether now. His parents eventually started noticing Griffin's reactions to building new family traditions. Together, they found ways to take some of the old traditions and blend them in with the new family. While it never quite felt the same, Griffin noticed that the traditions he now has with his new families are turning out to be cool, too. He started to recognize that even though change was hard, it often led to developing new relationships that he didn't expect and really enjoyed.

What Are Expectations?

Expectations are those tricky things we believe should or will happen in our relationships with ourselves, others, and the world around us. Sometimes we are conscious of our expectations, but most of the time we are not. We usually realize our expectations through disappointment or excitement for how things turned out. It is important to learn our expectations, because otherwise we can potentially go through life learning about relationships in an unrealistic way that is super hard to change.

In this exercise, think back on a time when you felt really disappointed in how something turned out. For example, you were spending time with one parent and their new partner and kids for the holidays. You and your parent have always watched the same movie at this time of year, but the other family members didn't want to watch it, so you all watched something else. The expectation you had is that the traditions you've grown up knowing would always stay the same. Use the following lines to write out your memory and what you think your underlying expectation was.

_____

_____

_____

_____

_____

_____

_____

_____

_____

_____

_____

Do My Expectations Need to Change?

If I'm constantly disappointed in something, to the point I want to avoid it altogether, then something may need to change. Change is a good thing, even though it doesn't always feel like it in the moment. Change is inevitable, and that's why it often sparks grief, resentment, or hope.

In this exercise, write some of the things that have been happening to you, and with whom, that have caused disappointment, resentment, or the desire to avoid them in the first column. In the second column, write how you may want to create some flexibility and openness for change in expectations.

I usually find myself getting disappointed or frustrated because I expect that things will be done a certain way, stay the way they've always been, or happen according to my timing. Life doesn't work like that, and living in a blended family is going to cause some of these issues to come to the surface. Even though you may not have wanted this change, know that it is preparing you to deal with unexpected and unwanted change throughout the rest of your life. This exercise will help you create more flexibility in how things could or should be. I'll give you an example:

CURRENT EXPECTATION	FLEXIBLE EXPECTATION
I get things done in my time.	*I will need to do things when I'm not always ready because it's needed.*

Learn to Check in with Your Expectations

Unmet expectations are hard to deal with. On the other hand, things turning out better than you expected can feel unbelievable. Our brains like to focus on all the things that are not going the way we want and use that information to keep us from getting our hopes up in the future. Our brains can even take great information and formulate even higher expectations of perfection on future experiences.

In this next exercise, you will compare your expectations with reality and record them in a grid. The next time you know you're leaving your house, even if it's going to school, practice, or a friend's house, think about what you expect will happen when you go do that activity. Think about the people you will be with and how you expect those interactions to go. What people will be there, and how do you expect those interactions to go? What feelings might you have, and how do you expect yourself to respond to the situation? You will write those expectations in the following chart. When you come home, write how you actually felt, who was around you, and what your reactions were. You can use this exercise as a way to track if your expectations may need to change or if you may need to set more boundaries, which we will talk about later in this chapter.

DATE	EXPECTATIONS	REALITY

Practicing Empathy

We all need to get into the habit of noticing and being aware of how other people are doing the best they can. Because we are human, we are all going to hurt and disappoint one another. Next time someone disappoints you or forgets something that is important, before you respond to them, try to think in your head, *Maybe this person is doing the best they can right now*. Engaging in this practice will slow down your response and make it more thoughtful.

Practicing Gratitude When Life Gets Messy

Things are never going to go the way we expect them to all the time. We have to learn to evaluate our expectations constantly but not let disappointment get the better of us. I find it extremely helpful to practice a little gratitude when things don't go as expected. I might say to myself, *You tried your best* or *I'm glad I learned something new*. Having difficult emotions is just as valid as experiencing happier moments and feelings. They both are necessary and normal parts of the human experience. However, we have to support ourselves in cultivating a life of gratitude or we will learn to self-protect and not trust anyone or anything.

Lessons Learned

You have already been through so much in your life. I know that it's scary when change happens that you can't control or predict. I want you to remember that you have survived 100 percent of what life has thrown at you so far. Think about all that you have learned and the things you have done to adapt to the change in your life. Maybe some of it's good and some of it's bad, but I want you to take this opportunity to notice how you have tried and survived.

_____

_____

_____

_____

_____

_____

_____

_____

_____

_____

_____

_____

_____

_____

_____

_____

_____

What Are Boundaries?

Healthy relationships require healthy boundaries. Boundaries are what we teach people about how to treat us and interact with us. To simplify it even more, boundaries are what is okay versus what is not okay. In your next conversation with a parent, stepsibling, or friend, pay close attention to the interaction. Ask yourself, *What about this interaction is okay? What about this interaction didn't feel okay?* This is a helpful way to check in with yourself and evaluate a situation to see if your boundaries are being maintained or if a conversation needs to be had. In order to set a boundary, you have to know what your boundaries are and when and by whom they're being crossed. In this exercise, you'll recall a recent interaction to determine how your boundaries were crossed.

Choose a recent event where you feel your boundaries were crossed. First ask yourself, *What was okay about this situation or experience for me?* For example, *It's okay that this person has emotions,* or *It's okay to be given extra work.*

Next think about what wasn't okay for you in this same situation. For example, *It wasn't okay to yell and curse at me, making me feel worthless* or *I will only do extra work if it doesn't interfere with my school schedule or practices.*

Using this information, fill in the boxes below.

THIS WAS OKAY	THIS WAS NOT OKAY

How and When to Share a Boundary

Some boundaries need to be shared verbally with people who either don't know your boundaries or who have crossed your boundaries. People who love and care about you will want to know and respect them, even if they don't agree with them. There are some people who don't even know their own boundaries and will feel threatened by you setting yours. That doesn't make your boundaries any less important.

Sometimes setting boundaries will cause you to lose people in your life, and that is okay. Boundaries are a form of protection, and having them heard and respected is necessary in a healthy relationship. Sometimes these boundaries have to be communicated to a person who is hurting you. Other times a boundary can be set by no longer engaging in certain conversations or activities without any explanation. In other words, you pull your energy, time, and resources away from that person or situation.

Learning to set boundaries is tricky, constantly changing, and requires lifelong practice. For this exercise, you will think of ways a boundary can be shared verbally and write a few ideas. Then think of ways a boundary can be shared nonverbally and add those to the chart. I'll give you some ideas as well.

HOW TO SET A BOUNDARY VERBALLY	HOW TO SET A BOUNDARY NONVERBALLY
"I know you were being playful, but please don't make comments about my body."	*Walk away*
"If your plans change, please let me know ahead of time."	*Make no eye contact*
"No."	*Do not respond to text*

It Goes Both Ways

You are learning and sharing your boundaries. I assure you that the people in your life, like your parents, teachers, and siblings, are trying to do the same because of the transition you're going through. For this exercise, I want you to identify an adult in your life to whom you can talk. Interview them about what they believe boundaries are and how they have been working to set boundaries. If you're up for it, ask them what they think their boundaries are with you and how they have shared them either verbally or nonverbally.

We need to learn from those who have gone before us. Take from the lessons they've already had to learn. You don't always have to do things the hard way to get the lessons you need. A good mentor will teach you their experiences and also ask you questions to better understand your own. In the space provided, write some of the lessons you learned from that interview to review later when you need some inspiration or support.

Support When Setting and Keeping Boundaries Gets Hard

Journaling is always a good idea, but if you really don't like journaling, have a trusted friend, parent, or therapist help you process boundary-setting. You can explore what boundaries you'd like to set, what emotions come up when you think about setting that boundary, and if that boundary is something that needs to be verbally communicated or is just an activity or conversation you don't have to give energy to. You can rely on your journal or trusted person for accountability and support during the entire process of identifying boundaries, setting them, and the reactions you receive. As I mentioned before, boundaries are messy. You are going to feel bad and guilty sometimes even though you know you are doing the right thing. You will need a safe person to talk to evaluate your boundaries and how implementing them is going.

Boundaries Check-In

As you've been learning about boundaries, I want you to think about what feelings come up for you. Many people feel fearful and anxious about setting boundaries and how it will impact them and their relationships. Setting boundaries can be scary because it's teaching people to treat you differently than they have, and people can get upset by that. What does taking small and manageable steps look like for you when it comes to boundary-setting? You don't have to start setting boundaries with everyone and in every situation to be making progress. Maybe start with one person or try one situation during the week, and check in with how you feel using the tools you've learned.

_____

_____

_____

_____

_____

_____

Developing Trust

Trust is something that develops over time based on the consistency of your interactions with someone else. Trust can also be torn down overnight. When we trust someone, we have had consistent experiences with them that let us know it's safe to share certain information or have expectations around loyalty and follow-through. Trust does require you to take some risks at the beginning in order to see if a person is worthy of your trust. If you've been hurt badly before, the idea of taking a risk on someone new or trusting someone who has hurt you again is scary.

For this exercise, I want you to write down the names of people you trust in three different categories.

1. In the smallest circle, write the name(s) of people you would share very personal information with or rely on heavily in a time of need.

2. In the middle circle, write the name(s) of people who you are beginning to build trust with and enjoy spending time with.

3. In the outer circle, write the name(s) of people you spend time with or know but don't trust with very personal information or expectations of need.

This exercise can help you identify how much you trust people and to see how one person might move from the outer circle to an inner circle. You can come back to this exercise time and time again to assess who you trust and who you'd like to trust more. Trust can be built over time when two people take a mutual risk to confide in each other and see how it goes.

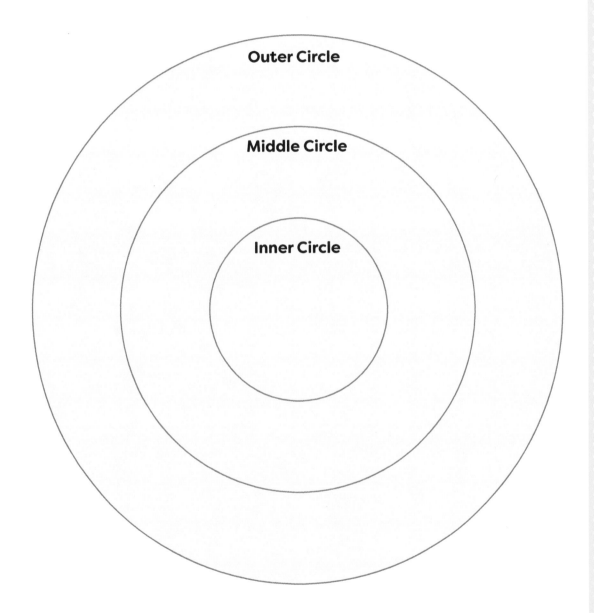

Outer Circle

Middle Circle

Inner Circle

Relationships Take Curiosity and Risk

Let's dig a little bit deeper. In this exercise, you will revisit the names from the "Developing Trust" exercise (page 84) and write down your findings about each. Think of the person or people whose name you put in the smallest circle, and write down how they got there—how did they earn your trust? Think about what they do or have done that lets you know they can be trusted. Next think of the people who are in the middle circle: What has kept them from moving into the inner circle, and how might you grow and develop those relationships to build trust? Finally, think of the people you put in the largest circle. What keeps them there? Are there any of those people you'd like to move to the middle circle, and how? Write your responses for each person in the space beside their name.

I encourage you to include at least one or two parents, stepparents, or new siblings in this exercise so you can work on being curious about them and giving them opportunities to build trust with you. Next pick a family member from the list, and think about what you want to ask them or see in their behavior that would let you know they are a trustworthy person. Once you have come up with what you'd like to see or hear from them in order to build trust, put forth some vulnerability, and ask those questions to get to know them or arrange another activity to get to know them like playing a game, grabbing a coffee, or making a TikTok video together.

Make the Time to Spend Some Time

You may have mixed feelings about getting to know your new family, but it's important to be positive and put forth real effort in getting to know the people in your life. It will make things more comfortable for everyone. You can absolutely start off small and at any step you are comfortable with. I want you to think of one way you can engage with your new family members consistently during the weeks that you are together. Write their individual names in the chart, and then write one way you can connect with them every week. This could be as simple as asking a new sibling about their day. (See my example below.) Remember that trust is built over time and through consistency. You have to put in as much effort as much as you want them to put in.

NAME	ACTIVITY/ENGAGEMENT
Jonah	*Ask how his day is going*

End of the Week Check-In

I'm a big fan of regularly checking in with yourself as you're trying new things. I've thrown a lot of new tools and ideas your way, and I know I've pushed you outside your comfort zone. Good! You can't grow without being a little bit nervous. Checking in at the end of every week regarding the things you've tried will help you evaluate what's working, what's not working, and how you're feeling about all of it. You can do this check-in by writing in a journal, sitting with your thoughts, or talking with a trusted friend or therapist.

Adding Fun into Growing Relationships

I don't know about you, but if I have to build a relationship with someone, I want to at least be having fun. Think about things you really enjoy doing, and try asking one of your family members to do something with you. I want you to let them know you want to build a relationship with them. You can definitely say it in your own words! If people know what you're trying to accomplish, they might be more open to going along with the activity and may even try to reach out to you in their own way to connect. I know this is hard and it may seem a little daunting, but you've got this. Vulnerability and risk are a hard reality for trust and relationship building. To be honest, most people are just as nervous as you when it comes to building relationships, even if you can't tell. Trust this therapist—we all are!

Creating Healthy Relationships

Think about what it will take for you to have the life and relationships you want. I know it's easier to think of being alone or not taking the risk. However, we are all designed to really crave connection. Write the vision you had in your head, and use it to remind yourself if or when things get difficult.

_____

_____

_____

_____

_____

_____

_____

_____

_____

_____

_____

_____

_____

_____

_____

_____

_____

_____

Amiika's Story

Amiika was really popular and didn't find making new friends very challenging. What she did find extremely challenging was investing effort into getting to know her new stepmom. She would give one-word answers at dinner and bow out of every opportunity for one-on-one time with her stepmom. She knew at some point they'd have to develop some kind of a relationship. As she explored her own resistance to developing a relationship with her stepmom, she realized that she was afraid of what her biological mom might think about her having a relationship with her stepmom. She told her mom her fears and realized that everyone wanted her to be happy and at least try to have a relationship with her stepmom. Amiika started out by answering the questions asked of her over dinner with a little more thought. She eventually invited her stepmom to see a movie. Their relationship is still growing slowly, but Amiika has found that she can take her time, check in with her feelings, create boundaries, and set realistic expectations about what this relationship with her stepmom will really look like for her now and in the near future. She doesn't need another mother—she just wants there to be comfort in the interactions between her and her stepmom at home.

WRAP-UP

We've learned that change is messy, and learning and setting healthy boundaries and expectations is a lifelong process. Take the pressure off of yourself to have it all figured out now and what things will look like in the future. You've got to take this one day at a time. If something is working, keep doing it. If something isn't working, you don't have to keep doing it. Definitely check in with why you think it's not working and if it needs adjustment before cutting out the practice completely.

CHAPTER 5

Communication Is Key

Communication is the foundation to any relationship. Without it, you can't really know yourself or another person. In this chapter, you will learn to figure out who you are, what you feel, what you need, and clear strategies and tools for communicating those things to others. A new family dynamic makes everything more challenging, so as you move through this chapter, remember that all of you are learning and growing. Learning to communicate will be messy and hard but so worth it in the long run.

Ben's Story

Ben found that he often felt guilty for all the fighting between his parents. He believed that by not getting the best grades or by making mistakes that he was the reason why his parents couldn't get along. His parents ended up divorcing, and within a year, both of them were remarried. His whole life changed, and he couldn't get past the feeling that it was his fault his parents split up. He felt very sad and often alienated himself from his friends and family because he didn't want to ruin any other relationships. His mother eventually sent him to a therapist to work through what he was feeling. He realized that he was holding responsibility for his parents' choices and knew it was time to talk to them. He sat down with both his parents and shared what he had been feeling. His parents were able to reassure him that their divorce was not his fault and that he could always talk to them about anything he was feeling. With a lot of work and time, Ben was able to rebuild his self-confidence and develop new friendships again.

Who Are We Talking To?

It is time to get clear on who you are wanting to talk to in your life and why. Usually we hold on to hard feelings and issues for way too long. The cycles that we hate continue to further the resentment and pain we feel. Remember, your life has changed dramatically, and the sooner you identify who you have your biggest issue with and find the courage and words to talk to them, the sooner you can find the peace you need within yourself and hopefully in that relationship.

You may feel like you are having issues with multiple people in your life, but usually there are just one to two individuals who are the root of the issue. This could be your parents, yourself, a stepparent, or a stepsibling. In my experience, we tend to hold a lot of anger at our parents or ourselves for the change in our lives. The way you can identify who you need to have a conversation with most is figuring out who you blame for the pain and changes in your life.

1. Who do you need to have a conversation with?

_____

Next think about why you blame them for the pain or changes in your life. Think about the decisions they made, the things they said, and the things they did or did not do that you feel should have or should not have been done, and write them down.

2. What was said, done, or not done that caused you pain?

Example: *When you pulled me from my school and made me move into a new home with people I don't even like or know.*

_____

_____

_____

If there are multiple people you feel have caused you pain, start with one person, and you can repeat this exercise for the others. Try not to overwhelm yourself with all the conversations that may need to be had, and focus on the ones you think about most often or that impact your life on a frequent basis. We will follow up on next steps in the next exercise. It's good to start with identifying the person and the issue, so take your time with finding clarity on the person and the issue.

What Am I Hoping Will Come from This?

Making the decision to bring an issue to someone first requires an understanding of what you hope to achieve from the conversation. Make sure that whatever you hope to gain can come directly from you. We can't control the behaviors, thoughts, or intentions of others. We can be really disappointed if we're always waiting for another person to give us what we need.

For example, if you are hoping for an apology to make the conversation seem worth it or successful, I would encourage you to consider that sharing your feelings and communicating your boundaries to a person who has hurt you are far better outcomes because these lie within your control. You may really need and deserve an apology, and I hope that you receive one. However, it's more productive to focus on building your communication skills by identifying your feelings, setting your boundaries, and getting clear on your expectations for how people treat you. So the first step is identifying your ideal outcome.

1. Based on my answers in the "Who Are We Talking To?" exercise (page 95), what do I wish would come from this conversation?

Example: *I wish I could go back to my old school and live with my other parent.*

_____

_____

_____

_____

_____

_____

_____

Next we are going to focus on what is within your control to either give in this conversation or to clarify. You may want to think of exactly what you would like to say to this person. Remember to keep the focus on what you can control.

2. What do you want to say? Write down with clarity what is within your control based on what is communicated, how it's communicated, and what your next steps after this conversation will be.

Example: *I want to let my parent know my feelings of anger and hurt and clearly express my need for a sense of control and at least have my voice heard when it comes to changes that will impact my life.*

_____

_____

_____

_____

_____

_____

_____

We will put all this together in the next exercise and discuss how you can practice clearly communicating everything you've written here. This is a difficult topic to tackle, so be patient with yourself as you practice putting everything you've done all together. Communication skills are intentionally developed and don't usually come naturally. You can only get better the more you practice.

Put It All Together

We've been through a lot in the last two exercises, so now let's bring it all together. I've always felt that it's not about how much you say but about how clearly you say it. How we start a conversation will usually dictate the outcome. Nobody likes to be addressed with anger and blame. I want to make sure your voice gets heard because it is important. These are skills I wish were taught to me when I was younger because they can save so much heartache and pain.

This exercise will test your skills from the previous chapters about naming emotions, identifying where those emotions come from, and exploring positively stated needs. We will also use the information you've written in the previous two exercises and put it all together in a clear statement you can present to the person you want to talk to. I call this exercise the softened start-up.

A softened start-up is "I feel_____ about _____.

I need_____."

Let's get started using your examples from the "Who Are We Talking To?" (page 95) and "What Am I Hoping Will Come from This?" (page 96) exercises.

1. Write down the emotions that come to the surface from the person you identified in the "Who Are We Talking To?" exercise (page 95).

I feel _____

Example: *I feel angry, hurt, not considered, out of control, powerless, helpless, etc.*

_____

_____

2. Write down what brought up these emotions for you. Try not to use "you" statements that place blame on the other person. I know you do feel some blame, but the focus is to keep this about you and the impact of the change to you.

About _____

Example: *About experiencing a major change without warning to my everyday life like friends, home, and school. I didn't feel like I had any say or that my voice heard at all.*

_____

_____

_____

3. Look back at step 2 from the "What Am I Hoping Will Come from This?" exercise (page 97), and write it down here.

I need _____

Example: *I need to share my feelings with you and know that I've clearly communicated my need to have my voice heard when it comes to changes that will impact my everyday life.*

_____

_____

_____

Finally, you can practice saying all three steps together in that order to the person you identified in the "Who Are We Talking To?" exercise (page 95).

Talking Things Through

Thinking about who you need to talk to, why, and your ideal outcome is probably pretty scary and overwhelming. Think about your worst-case scenario when having this conversation. For example, you may think, *This person will laugh at me or judge me.* Next we'll learn a practice for navigating worst-case scenarios.

_____

_____

_____

_____

_____

_____

_____

_____

_____

_____

_____

_____

_____

_____

_____

_____

_____

_____

_____

_____

_____

Game Plan for Worst-Case Scenarios

We all imagine worst-case scenarios when making a decision. Most of the time our worst-case scenario doesn't happen, but sometimes it does. In order to keep yourself from getting stuck, identify how you would go about handling the worst-case scenario if it happens. Having a plan and seeing that you can and will get through it can help reduce anxiety and keep you from getting stuck. For example, if your biggest fear is that they will judge you, think about how you might handle that. You may start with thanking them for your time, then going home and practicing breathing, saying something kind to yourself, and then journaling how that experience made you feel. Finally, you might pick a different accountability partner and start by sharing with them a little bit of your story to see their response.

Feeling Scared Is a Sign You're Growing

We often think we have to go into difficult conversations with a lot of confidence and without fear. The truth is that we will usually feel pretty scared when it comes to vulnerably sharing our feelings with someone who has hurt us. We don't always know if the outcome will turn out well or if anything will change. I want you to define confidence as feeling the fear and doing what needs to be done and saying what needs to be said anyway, regardless of the outcome. Not everyone will like what you have to say, no matter how well you say it. The goal is to be proud of yourself because you identified something as painful and set a boundary. Remember, you can only control what you do.

Conflict Is Healthy

Most of us believe that having conflict with another person is a bad thing to avoid at all costs. The truth is, conflict is a natural and healthy part of any relationship. Conflict is inevitable. If we try to avoid it, we can end up losing ourselves in the context of any relationship. Plus, every person we are in a relationship with has different life experiences that shape how they view situations, circumstances, and expectations, and conflict is bound to arise. In this exercise, I want you to evaluate what you believe about conflict, where you learned it from, and how you would like to view conflict in light of what you are learning about yourself in this workbook.

1. What do you believe about conflict, and how would you define it?

_____

_____

_____

2. Where and from whom did you learn that about conflict?

_____

_____

_____

3. Write your new definition of conflict here based on what you're learning about yourself in this workbook. Use this as your mantra that you say to yourself when you know an issue needs to be addressed in the future.

_____

_____

_____

Identifying and Practicing Roles in Conflict

Have you ever been in an argument with someone and things just go round and round in circles? That is usually because you are both convinced that there is only one way to see a situation and you are trying to persuade the other person to see it the way you do. One of the things that I teach people in my counseling practice is that there are always two ways to view a situation, and each has validity or accuracy to the person sharing it. Your first task in a conflict situation, before problem-solving or persuading, is to listen with the goal of understanding and ask the other person to do the same for you. In the next few exercises, I will teach you what the next steps are once both people feel heard. First, I want you to get to know what a speaker does and what a listener does.

Speaker Role:

- Utilize the softened start-up outline you practiced in the "Who Are We Talking To?" (page 95), "What Am I Hoping Will Come from This?" (page 96), and "Put It All Together" (page 98) exercises.

- Talk only about yourself.

- Share what you may need or have needed when the situation occurred.

- Avoid blame.

Listener Role:

- Put aside your own judgment of what the speaker is saying.

- Take notes.

- Ask open-ended questions (questions that can't be answered with a yes or no).

- Summarize what you heard the speaker say.

You can switch roles when the speaker feels heard and start the process again.

Learning the Art of Summarizing

People always hear better when they feel heard. If you want to get anywhere in a conversation with another person, especially when the topic is difficult, showcase that you heard what they are saying. Try using their own words and not sharing with them your interpretation of what they said. You don't want to add to what they said. This takes a lot of work to really tune into what the other person is saying and will take some practice to get good at.

Here are my steps for becoming a great listener and summarizing to someone in order to make them feel heard. If you have to talk to a parent or stepparent, you can get these directions out and read them together to make sure you are on the same page with what you are trying to accomplish.

1. Take notes in the lines below and write down direct quotes, specific words, or feelings used. You can download a podcast and practice this step by taking notes on a conversation that has nothing to do with you.

2. Use the softened start-up approach (page 98) when sharing information back.

   Example: *I heard you say you felt [sharing the emotions they used] because this is what you expected or how you saw this happening, and you need [share the needs they expressed].*

3. Check in with them to see if you heard correctly or if they would like to clarify anything.

_____

_____

_____

_____

_____

_____

_____

_____

Working through Conflict

I don't know about you, but all this talk about conflict has made me feel overwhelmed and tired. What feelings and desires did you feel as we worked through practicing having conflict? You may feel like scrolling social media, getting outside, or reading a book. Many of us enjoy distracting ourselves when conflict or the idea of having a hard conversation becomes overwhelming. Noticing these feelings can be a sign to you in the future that you may need to take a self-care break.

_____

_____

_____

_____

_____

_____

_____

_____

_____

_____

_____

_____

_____

_____

_____

_____

The Art of Digging Deeper

When we have an emotional or physical reaction to a situation or experience, our bodies are trying to tell us that they have a story from our past that relates to this. Most of us aren't always conscious of what story from our past is driving our reactions.

Here are some questions that I regularly ask myself and my clients when exploring reactions to certain situations. The goal is to become conscious of why we react the way we do so we can communicate more clearly with others, set healthy boundaries, and set expectations that meet the present moment and person with whom we're interacting.

Please know that you won't always be able to know why you have some reactions, but you can trust that when a reaction happens, either physically or emotionally, you may want to self-soothe and practice some distracting activities that we've talked about before. Don't judge yourself for not understanding, but, if you're able in the moment, do try to ask yourself the following questions:

1. What does this situation tell me about my boundaries and expectations with this person?

_____

_____

_____

2. Do I remember feeling like this before? If so, when?

_____

_____

_____

3. What feelings are coming up for me right now? Use your emotional vocabulary sheet you created in the "Learn Your Emotions" exercise (page 36) in chapter 2.

_____

_____

_____

4. What would be my ideal dream for this situation or issue?

_____

_____

_____

5. What do I need in this situation?

_____

_____

_____

6. Do I have a fear or a disaster scenario playing through my mind?

_____

_____

_____

Asking yourself questions will help you understand yourself and your reactions better so you can make decisions in the future that support you in your needs and boundaries.

Staying Mindful in Conflict Discussions

Conflict can make anyone's heart beat faster, and those feelings we experience can feel uncontained. In this practice, I want you to pick three skills you can use when you are feeling overwhelmed. You can use many of the exercises you've already learned in this book. For example, do a deep-breathing exercise, distract yourself with music or art, or move your body in some way to reduce tension. Make sure the three things you choose help you to focus your attention on something other than the conflict discussion or the feelings you experience while in the conflict. Your system can't relax if your brain is still focused on the feelings and issues.

Learning How to Move Forward

To truly take a step forward, each person in the conversation needs to be able to identify their core needs around the issue or topic at hand. Core needs are things we cannot negotiate without losing a piece of ourselves. Next each of you will need to focus on the things you are more open to talking about or open to changing, like when something happens, how it happens, or who does it. Then you can both share your core needs and the things you are flexible about with one another. Write them down in the box.

CORE NEEDS	THINGS I'M FLEXIBLE ON

Next work together to answer the following questions:

What things do we agree on?

_____

_____

_____

What would a temporary or partial step forward look like if we were to focus on our areas of flexibility?

_____

_____

_____

When can we check back in on how this step went?

_____

_____

_____

This exercise works best when everyone feels heard and is prepared to work with one another. It will help you understand if this is a person who can truly have healthy conflict with you. If they can't, you may need to reassess boundaries and expectations. You're doing a lot of hard work to learn about and express yourself. These exercises offer you suggestions and structure, but you are also welcome to create your own questions and structure for what works for you.

Let Go of Tension

You deserve some time to move your body. After difficult conversations, our bodies usually hold the tension. Try some movement and stretching, like jumping jacks, moving your head from side to side, walking, running, or moving your shoulders up and down. As you move, think about letting go of the tension with one movement and imagine increasing in self-compassion as you practice another movement. For example, if you choose jumping jacks, you release the tension when your arms go up, and when your arms come back down, you increase the feeling of self-love.

It's Time to Have the Talk

It's the moment you've been preparing for throughout the chapter. You are going to have the talk with the person you identified in the "Who Are We Talking To?" exercise (page 95). You've done all the prep work, learned that confidence is doing something even when you're afraid, and have a clear way of expressing yourself. Before you have the talk, do a breathing exercise and have something nice planned for yourself after the conversation, like watching your favorite show or scrolling through social media. What I'm asking you to do is hard, but you are going to be light-years ahead of your peers in learning and practicing these tools. These tools should be practiced with adults in your life such as a parent or counselor who can be patient with you and open to hearing what you say. Also, as I've previously recommended, you can ask to read these directions aloud before starting so that your parent or whoever you identified to talk to can know what you're hoping to achieve.

Note of Encouragement

You've done some hard work, and it's time to send yourself a little encouragement to focus on all that you tried. Look at yourself in a mirror, and tell yourself five things you are proud of yourself for. It doesn't matter if you fully believe what you're saying about yourself right now. What matters is that you are intentionally speaking kindly to yourself as you're learning new things. Here are a few nice things you can say to yourself:

→ I'm proud of myself for learning something new.

→ I'm happy that I tried to express myself in a productive way.

→ I'm proud of myself for planning some self-care activities I enjoy.

→ I'm learning and that's enough.

Noticing How It Went

Reflect on the conversation you had. What were the things you felt were easy for you to do from the exercises you learned? What did you find difficult? How did you experience the other person's reaction? It's always helpful to reflect on how things go so you can continue to learn and grow.

_____

_____

_____

_____

_____

_____

_____

_____

_____

_____

_____

_____

_____

_____

_____

_____

_____

_____

_____

Skylar's Story

Skylar had been feeling angry at her dad for several months. She avoided being in the same room as him and his new partner. When she was at their house, all she did was count down the hours until she could go back to her mom's house. She realized she would eventually have to have a conversation with her dad about how she was feeling and focus on really understanding what she needed in order to feel more comfortable with her dad and his partner. After several days of journaling and meditation, she realized that she was really hurt that she had no say in how her life had changed and needed to be part of conversations about future changes. She sat down with her dad and expressed the need for being a part of conversations just to feel heard and understood even if it didn't change the outcome of the decision. Her dad was able to hear her emotions, and the two continue to work together to try to understand each other and talk about changes and choices together.

WRAP-UP

Learning to communicate is one of the hardest things to do as you move through change and transition into adulthood. You will find that most people don't know how to communicate effectively. Now that you have the tools, you can create positive change in your home and in your relationships. Be patient and gentle with yourself and others as everyone adapts to new ways of communicating. Remember that oftentimes everyone will have very different feelings and needs. Most of the time having one conversation won't solve things. In order to build relationships, you may have to have the same conversation over and over again as you learn about yourself and each other—especially because you are changing so much right now in this time of your life. What you need, feel, or want can change drastically in a short amount of time.

CHAPTER 6

Meet Your New Normal Head-On

This chapter will be your guide to putting together what you've learned, creating a plan, and practicing checking in with yourself and your progress toward your personal development. Connecting with your new family is going to take time. For some it will come easy, and for others it won't. Every family is different, and our reactions to being in a blended family can be very diverse. I hope that this chapter will teach you to have grace for yourself, think about who you are and who you want to become, and resist comparing your journey to someone else's.

Stephen's Story

Stephen was blindsided when his family split. Everything about his life changed. Some things he was excited to see change, and other aspects he dreaded. He now lives primarily with his mother and sees his father every other weekend. He used to do everything with his dad. It was really hard for him to understand what happened and why he couldn't see his dad as much as he wanted.

Stephen found influencers, teachers, and friends who had been through what he was going through. When things got tough, he had a network of support to reach out to. It didn't happen overnight, and learning to trust people was difficult at first. He also learned that music and art always helped him tap into his feelings, and those mediums became a way he could express himself when things got overwhelming. Stephen began learning how to play the guitar and writing music. That hobby was an outlet for his emotions and became the one thing that helped him the most through the change. It was something he could always count on. If he had a hard time expressing himself to his mentors and friends, he would share the music he had been writing. After several years, he began sharing his music in groups and found that others were able to connect to his stories and feel a little less alone in the world, too.

Eventually his mom remarried, and Stephen now has stepsiblings. The house is a little louder, and he has to make space for himself to practice his music. His room is where he goes to get away from it all and write his music.

Learning Yourself Is a Lifelong Journey

What you are learning and have learned in this workbook is just the beginning. I want you to think about how you may continue to invest in your own personal growth throughout your life. Consider how you best learn and grow. Is it through listening, watching, reading, or just doing something new?

In this exercise, you are going to write yourself a letter making a commitment to keep investing in your growth. Think about the things you have learned so far in terms of self-care, connecting with others, sharing your feelings, and finding new hobbies. In this letter, write down how you would like to put those tools and ideas into practice. For example, you may want to wake up at 8 a.m. every morning and develop a ritual of taking a shower, saying your affirmations, and doing a quick stretch.

The purpose of writing yourself this letter is to make a commitment to yourself and remind yourself of everything you've learned. When we write something down, we are more likely to follow through. There may be times in your life that you forget to develop yourself personally. Then you can remember the commitment you made to yourself, get back up, and try again.

Dear _____,

_____

_____

_____

_____

_____

Sincerely, _____

Practicing Grace

I love the idea that we can't practice hate or anger when we are actively trying to understand someone's story. Use moments of self-judgment as opportunities to remind yourself of your story.

Go to a mirror in your room or bathroom where you have some privacy. Look at yourself with love and compassion as you reflect upon your life. Remember the challenges you've overcome. Focus on all the good things you've been through and the people who have been a part of it. Remind yourself of how much you've learned, the people you've met, and everything that could lie ahead for you (a dream career, going to college, or meeting people from different parts of the world). You can even think about what it has been like to be part of a new and growing family, how you chose to love them, and how they chose to love you. Recite affirmations of your strength, courage, and determination to keep going.

Practicing grace is all about truly seeking to understand ourselves and other people without judgment. In the words of one of my favorite authors and influencers, Brené Brown: "People are hard to hate close up."

Sharing What We're Learning

One of the ways we cement information in our heads is by teaching others what we've learned and tried. I want to encourage you to share with someone in your life what you have tried that works for you and might work for them. It makes us feel better to help others and really showcase to ourselves how far we have come.

Keep in mind that not everyone is ready for advice, though. It is always thoughtful to ask the question, "May I share my thoughts/ideas/advice on this with you?" Some people may say yes and others no. Either answer is okay because that is an act of boundary-setting. By first asking if advice is welcome, you are signaling that you care about the other person's boundaries. Whether or not people want to hear your advice usually doesn't have anything to do with you; rather, it usually has to do with the other person's headspace.

Sometimes sharing what you've learned can happen on a bigger platform through music, social media, or sharing with a group. You get to be creative here.

Know Your Tools

Using the following checklist template, write down at least three strategies you've learned in this book and actually tried. Now take a little time to be honest with yourself about how trying those exercises went for you. Did you enjoy them, and were they helpful? Did the exercises create more anxiety for you, or maybe you didn't feel anything at all? Remember, we're just noticing our responses here and not judging those responses. The key is that you tried something for yourself!

Next write down three other activities you've learned in this book that you haven't tried yet but want to try. Think about what has stopped you from trying them. Do you notice any resistance to those exercises? Do you find yourself excited to try them? How are you going to add these exercises to your schedule in the next couple of weeks?

I want the first thing you notice to always be what you have done, and then focus on what you have yet to do. Usually we initially focus on all that we are not or have not done, and that can ruin our motivation. Also, just seeing a check mark next to something gives our brain a little happiness boost!

✓ _____

✓ _____

✓ _____

☐ _____

☐ _____

☐ _____

☐ _____

Choosing Yourself

When things get difficult, how do you want to show up for yourself? Tell yourself that you love yourself and that you will do what it takes to love yourself even better . . . just like you might tell a friend. What are some kind things you might say to a friend when they're worried about something or feeling bad about themselves? Try looking at yourself in the mirror and saying those kind things to your reflection!

_____

_____

_____

_____

_____

_____

_____

_____

_____

_____

_____

_____

_____

_____

_____

_____

Breathing Practice

Take a moment to sit quietly in your chair or on your bed. Without trying to challenge your breath, just notice it. Notice the rise of your chest as you inhale and feel the relaxation of your chest as it sinks back in when your breath releases out of your mouth or nose. You're not controlling your breath, just noticing it and being present in the moment. As you begin to follow your natural breathing rhythm, you can deepen it by counting to four while picturing going around the four corners of a box. Then you can exhale to the count of four while imagining those same four points of a box. Try doing this complete breathing pattern four times total.

Shake It Off

When you can't seem to shake a feeling of sadness, avoidance, or anxiety, or you find yourself avoiding a situation or conversation, try literally shaking off those feelings! Put on your favorite song or grab your favorite instrument, and move your body to the sound of the music. You can move your hands, your head, or your whole body, as long as you move.

We can get bogged down by all the information swirling in our heads. Moving our bodies can change our mindset, outlook, and feelings. It's even better if you can get another person in on the action. Create your own dance party! Don't cringe! I know you rock out to your own music, so just do it now and let's laugh about how ridiculous we feel together. Moving our bodies creates a change in our emotional state. Adding music to that gives your mind a different emotion to focus on, like happiness.

After you've finished dancing and moving your body, check back in with your emotional state. Think about how your emotions have changed since you started. Practice gratitude for being able to move and change your mood, having the ability and resources to do hard things, or having access to books and the internet that give you the information you need to write a paper.

Think Holistically

We are complex, and our bodies need different things at different times. Use the following grid to check in with your emotional, physical, social, and academic health. In each box, write down the things you are doing to support that aspect of your life. By doing this, you'll be able to see which aspects may need some extra focus and support.

For example, with emotional health, you might notice that you've been journaling regularly and practicing identifying your emotions. For your physical health, you stretch regularly and have been running the school track. Your relationships have been put on the back burner because you've been busy. You haven't spent time with your friends in a while, but you've been texting. You can also use the relationships box to think about how you're investing in your family. Finally, consider how you may be focusing on your academic life. Are you studying nightly and preparing in study groups for upcoming tests?

After you've done a quick check-in for each of these areas, notice if you need to refocus your attention to a particular part of your life.

Emotional Health	
Physical Health	
Relationships	
Academics	

Watch Your Mindset

It's helpful to regularly check in on what you're saying to yourself. Get out a sheet of paper and write, "Hey, you. Yes, you! How are you feeling about yourself?" Post this somewhere you regularly look, like your mirror. This prompt will help you catch self-critical thoughts earlier so you can deliberately choose what you want to believe about yourself. Don't save this one for later. Take a moment right now to write it down and make sure it goes up. Then grab some more sheets of paper and write down some nice things about yourself to put up in the same area.

I love a good reminder. Let's make sure these notes don't disappear over time. Write down your best affirmations here, where they'll have the power to remind you of what you love about yourself right here on the page.

_____

_____

_____

_____

_____

_____

_____

_____

_____

_____

_____

_____

Reflecting on the Changes in Your Life

How has being in a blended family changed your relationship with yourself in terms of your emotional health and relationships? As you reflect on your answer to that question, think about how that makes you feel. This check-in may reveal some conversations you want to have. As you reflect on this, notice any negative feelings that may come up and share a kind thought with yourself like, I've been trying my best *or* I'm still learning.

_____

_____

_____

_____

_____

_____

_____

_____

_____

_____

_____

_____

_____

_____

_____

_____

Practicing Comfort

Comfort is something we all need, as life can take its toll on us. In this exercise, you are going to find comfort through a warm beverage. Take five minutes to make your favorite warm beverage. It could be a hot cup of herbal tea or hot chocolate. Be mindful of how you're feeling and take some deep breaths. Holding that warm drink can give you a sense of peace and comfort. As you hold the warm cup, you may notice that your brain allows you to bring up more positive memories from your life. You can give yourself the opportunity to relive those memories and enjoy the positive feelings that come with them. If you need a little extra support, think about a moment when you felt happiest around your family recently and a moment when you were happiest with just yourself.

Finding Accountability

There are differences between having a mentor and having someone who holds you accountable. I have friends with whom I've shared my goals and feelings who regularly check in with me to see how I'm doing and to ask about my progress with my goals. Friends help me hold myself accountable.

A mentor is someone who represents who we want to be or has been through what we're going through and has navigated it well. They are someone who inspires us to do better and helps influence us toward becoming our best selves.

Mentors also challenge us to grow and try new things. Mentors can come from all different parts of our lives, like school, sports, or religious activities. Having a few mentors or people we look up to will give us a road map for how we may want to show up in our lives and the community in a way that makes us feel good and makes a difference in the lives of others. Accountability from a mentor helps us stay true to the things we really want for our lives. Holding ourselves accountable can be tricky because our feelings don't always match our long-term desire. The accountability from a mentor is a way to make sure we follow through on the goals and things we say are important to us.

Build Your Community

Who you spend your time with largely impacts your life and future choices. In this exercise, you'll focus on identifying the people in your life who make you feel happy and what you're doing with them when you feel the happiest and most connected. Write their names in the circle provided. You may only have one or two people whose names you'd write down here. That is great! Close contacts who have a big impact on us are rare. Also think about the good things they bring to your life and how they support you in learning about yourself and being your best self.

   Now you are going to send them a text or write them a letter to tell them how you feel about them. If you're old school like me, you can even write them a handwritten letter about how they've impacted your life in a positive way. Acknowledging the people in your life and letting them know how you feel about them will help them feel loved and appreciated and help you feel better, too.

Date Yourself

The sooner you learn to enjoy your own company, the better. Think about it—you'll have more to share when you're with others and will be more discerning about who you let into your life. Don't get me wrong, I want you to have friends and enjoy your time with them, but I also want you to enjoy and be intentional around the time you spend with yourself.

Depending on where you live, your budget, and the time you can spend on this, plan a perfect day or period of time that you can spend with just yourself. Then you have to make it happen with a plan and intentionality. Think about if you need to get approval from your family on the activity or budget. Maybe you have to shop for your favorite treats at the store. Your activity may take some planning, but it doesn't have to be constrained by money. Be creative and figure out what you need to do to make it happen.

Date: _____

Invite list: Me, myself, and I!

Idea: _____

_____

Location: _____

_____

Menu: _____

_____

Supplies: _____

_____

Budget: _____

_____

Permission: _____

_____

Find a Mentor

We all need someone we can look up to. Someone who has been through what we've been through, who can help us with insight and practical tips for navigating those seasons of our lives. This can be a person whom you interact with frequently or someone you read about in a book, magazine, or on social media. What is it about them that you look up to? How do you connect with them regularly to inspire yourself?

For this exercise, write down who your mentors are and fill in the answers to the questions. You can come back to this exercise to remind yourself of who you want to be, what you can do to practice that, and to check in with your mentor or learn more about them. You can even use this as a visualization exercise by envisioning your mentor and how they might deal with the situation you're dealing with—thinking about what they might say or how they might act and using that as a road map.

Who are your mentors?

_____

_____

Why do you look up to them?

_____

_____

How do you interact with them? How often?

_____

_____

If you do not personally know them, how often would you like to interact with them?

_____

_____

Mission Statement

Write a mission statement for how you will try to build your confidence and believe in yourself every day. You can think about the people in your life whom you admire and borrow some of the practices or sayings they use to help themselves in this area, too.

_____

_____

_____

_____

_____

_____

_____

_____

_____

_____

_____

Stretch to Release Tension

Whether you are sitting or standing, raise your hands above your head. Then move both arms toward the right side of your body and enjoy a nice stretch through the left side of your stomach. Now move both arms toward the left side of your body, noticing the same stretching sensation. Next put your hands on your hips and rotate your upper half toward the right and then again toward the left. These are great stretches for releasing tension and refocusing yourself.

Samantha's Story

Samantha loves her new stepfamily and wants to spend time with them. Her mom dated her stepdad for a long time before they got married, and she loves her stepsiblings. She always thought they were so cute when they were little. Samantha knows that she still needs to do things to stay in touch with herself, which means having some alone time at home. She strongly believes in staying active and always enjoys going for runs and practicing yoga at home with the help of YouTube videos. She used to have her siblings join in but decided that several nights a week she would keep this time just for herself to set healthy boundaries and stay focused on her self-care. She told her family ahead of time that she would be doing these things for herself, and they were supportive of her decision.

WRAP-UP

You've learned so many new tools. Hopefully some have been helpful to you, and it's okay if there are some you're still working through. The goal of this entire workbook is to give you insight and options as you navigate the road ahead in your blended family. Remember: take only what you need and want from this book. You can use this workbook to regularly check in with yourself by coming back to the exercises that align with what you're going through. That is why everything has been structured to help you easily identify what areas you may need to focus on first. Return to this workbook as needed for support in identifying your emotions, practicing self-care, and adding to and sharpening your communication tools.

PART III

Real-Life Q&A

Can you believe you've made it through this entire workbook already? I'm so proud of you! I know that working through these types of emotions, exercises, and prompts can be really challenging to fit into an already full schedule. You chose to learn and grow personally, and that takes a lot of determination and courage. In this final section of the workbook, I'll be answering questions from teens like you and providing additional exercises, practices, tools, and advice to navigate the challenges of blended family life.

Q: I feel really anxious and sad whenever I'm around my "new" family. I feel like an outsider who doesn't know where they belong. I miss the old days with both my parents. We used to have so much fun together.

A: Change is challenging, and it's normal for us to want what we once had. That longing is our mind's way of coping with big feelings and events we can't change. Our brains naturally want to take us back to the last place and time where we felt happy and secure. Learning your role and identity in this "new" family takes time and may require you to process some grief or sadness over the loss of your "old" family. First, talking with a parent, counselor, or friend to identify what emotions this change in your life brings will help you understand what you may need. Second, we can explore some of the times or ways when we do feel like someone in our new family is trying to make an effort to connect with us or how we're making an effort to connect with them. Finally, allow yourself to be in the same room with your family for at least five minutes each day and build on that time as you watch your emotions take shape. You may have to look for new ways to connect with your stepfamily, knowing that everything new you try will come with some awkwardness and fear.

Q: Am I the reason my mom and stepdad fight sometimes? I feel like they argue more and more ever since they got married a year ago. I can't go through another divorce.

A: Adults argue, and that can sometimes cause a lot of anxiety for the teens or children listening to it. You have gone through so much change recently, and you don't want to have to go through more. Your mom and stepdad fight for probably a variety of reasons, as they are trying to blend their lives together. Arguing between a couple is normal and is usually not a cause for concern. If the arguing is consistent or disruptive to you emotionally or physically, it may be a good idea to talk with your mom about your feelings and fears and ask for reassurance if that is what you need. You can also try putting on music to distract yourself and utilize any of the breathing or visualization exercises you learned in this workbook if you find your anxiety increasing during your parents' arguments.

Q: I really want to bond with my half brother, but he spends most of his time at his mom's house. I don't think he wants to put any effort into our relationship. Should I give up?

A: Wanting to build a relationship with a half brother or sister is a wonderful and healthy desire. Just like you, they may be struggling with the end of their parents' relationship and the beginning of a new one. As much as you may try to build a relationship, they may not want it, and that is okay. However, building a relationship takes time, and even if you feel rejection in the beginning, remind yourself that their desire for distance doesn't really have to do with you. Try to find small ways to connect through either a shared hobby or shared experience with the family. Allow the relationship to take its time to build. You can mitigate discouragement by managing your expectations for the relationship. An expectation is what we anticipate something should or will look like. If you manage your expectations in a realistic way to acknowledge that the relationship will take time and small moments of connection, which are just as important as big moments, you will hopefully notice a decrease in discouragement.

Q: My dad's new partner wants to be a part of every decision he makes for me about my allowance, how I get disciplined, and where I'm allowed to go. It's making it really hard for me to connect with them. Is that normal?

A: The beginning of any relationship is fragile, and developing a sense of trust and connection will take time. It has been my experience in cases like this that the stepparent is trying to become a parent to you as quickly as possible. They may be nervous or anxious, too, about building their home and a relationship with you. The best place to start is with acknowledging how you feel, then get curious about what emotions your stepparent may be feeling. Practice empathy for both them and yourself for this change in your lives, then talk about it with your dad. Ultimately, he will be the one to relay this information to your stepparent and change the expectations and boundaries around how decisions are made. If things seem to not get better after a couple months, it may be helpful to request family counseling to make it safer for all of you to share your feelings and set healthier, more realistic expectations. You can even try asking for time alone with your stepparent to do fun things only and see how well they respond to that. Having more fun together may open the lines of communication in the future for the two of you to explore your feelings and needs. I know you've heard me say this a lot in the workbook, but change takes time and requires needs to be clearly stated. Think and communicate from the perspective of what you do want instead of focusing only on what you don't want.

Q: I often want to be alone in my room. I don't really want to be at my mom and stepdad's house anymore. It's noisy and I barely get any privacy. They keep asking me to be a part of things, and we fight about how much time I spend alone. How do I talk to my mom about this without hurting her feelings?

A: Whenever we share our feelings and needs, we may hurt the feelings of others. We can't always avoid our parents' or half siblings' difficult reactions to our feelings. It sounds like you have a real need for privacy and alone time, which are boundaries that help you with self-care. By my definition, a boundary is teaching other people how to love you best. However, you need to acknowledge that other people have feelings as well. You can lovingly sit down with your parents and share with them what you are feeling, where those feelings are coming from, and what you need from them in order to feel comfortable in your home. After sharing those things, it will be helpful to verbally acknowledge that you understand they have different feelings from you and you'd like to hear those. Remember, someone else's feelings or needs do not invalidate your own. Two people can see and feel the same experience very differently. The goal of any beginning to a conversation is to understand and not try to fight for who is right. If you find communicating with your parents difficult, even when using all these tools, it may be time for support from another family member, family friend, or therapist to mediate.

Q: I really like my half sister and want to connect with her. She seems open to connecting, but our age difference makes it really hard to find things to do together. What are some ways to connect when you're really far apart in age?

A: Age differences can be tough. I remember really looking up to my older half sister. I wanted to spend as much time with her as I could. You can connect in simple ways through a show, a shared activity, or expressing curiosity about their world. Because of the age difference, it may be difficult to spend much time together, so aim to enjoy the moments that you do have. This goes back to having realistic expectations about what can and can't happen in any given relationship. Notice your feelings without judgment, and think about how much time you would want to spend with a younger sibling if they had the same age gap as you and your older half sibling. Think about easy ways to connect, like sharing a joke or remembering something that was important to them. Maybe try opening up about things that are important to you. It wouldn't hurt to ask your half sibling to hang out at a specific time to do a specific activity.

Q: I feel angry all the time. Even though I don't want to lash out at my mom and her new partner, it seems to come out of nowhere. I don't know how to control the anger and figure out why I'm so mad. Is this normal?

A: Anger is a healthy and natural emotion that everyone feels. It's often a protective emotion that keeps you from noticing other emotions like fear, sadness, or grief. It is what we do with that emotion of anger that matters. It is okay that you can't always articulate how you feel or what you might need. Many individuals don't even know how to do that in adulthood. Give yourself grace and acknowledge that what you're going through is difficult even if you don't understand it. If your anger persists for more than two weeks or a month, it could be a sign you need to talk to someone who can help you better understand what is happening inside you and what support you may need, like a counselor. Try walking yourself through mindfulness exercises like picturing your favorite place and noticing all the sights and smells around you. You can practice breathing exercises as well by just noticing the rise and fall of your chest as you breathe in and out. Journaling is also a great exercise to track your emotions associated with the events of each day and identify patterns or themes that you may need support to deal with.

Q: I feel like I'm being asked to do a million things when I'm at my mom's house, and it's much more peaceful at my dad's house. I don't want to hurt my mom's feelings, but I'd rather spend more time at my dad's house. I want to talk to my mom about how much she expects of me, but all I hear her tell me is how much was expected of her when she was my age and that I should be grateful. What can I do?

A: It sounds like when you try to bring up your feelings with your mom, you often feel unheard or put down. That really hurts, and I know that trying to change these situations can feel hopeless. The first thing to note is that your feelings are valid and important. Next try noticing how different the living situation is at your mom's house versus your dad's house. Are there more people living at your mom's house? Is the house bigger? Answering yes to those questions might mean that each person in the house is feeling the weight of all the needs of the household and everyone has to step up. Finally, think about what being asked to do all these things takes away from you. Are you finding that you're more stressed about your homework? Do you often feel tired, like you're not getting enough downtime? Think about what responsibilities you can handle on a daily basis, what you cannot handle on a daily basis, and how to better communicate to your mom what you can and can't do. It may make you seem more willing to collaborate and do your fair share rather than looking like you're trying to get out of chores. Try saying something like, "I've been really stressed out about schoolwork lately. I'm happy to do the dishes after dinner, but I need more time before dinner to focus solely on my homework."

Q: My stepdad is trying really hard to connect with me, but I think he believes he can replace my dad. I know I don't see my dad very often, but I don't want this guy thinking he can just come in and be my dad. How do I set limits and boundaries with him without hurting his feelings?

A: I think it's important to note that many stepparents understand that they can't take the place of a biological parent. Most of the time they want to connect and just aren't sure how to do it. Believe it or not, they feel anxiety around this topic as much as you do. Focus on communicating to them what things they can do with you. Setting boundaries in this case can be more focused on what is okay rather than only communicating what is not okay. Assume that they know they can't replace a parent when you go into any conversation with them. How we perceive a situation or someone's intention often dictates how we act around them. Assuming the best and then teaching them how to connect with you will often make things get better faster. Sit down and think about the things you do like doing with them or things you have talked about doing. What about those things do you like, and what about those things do you not like? For example, you may really like going to get ice cream and see a movie with your stepdad, but a certain ice cream place or genre of movie may be kept just between you and your biological dad.

Q: My mom just had her first baby with my stepdad. I often feel neglected whenever I'm at their house, like I'm some unwanted houseguest. They never tell me that, but it's how I feel. I don't know how to get past it, and I'm starting to not want to be there. What can I do?

A: This is a tough one because new babies do require a lot of attention, but that doesn't mean you don't deserve attention as well. I think it's very normal to feel neglected and wonder if you're even wanted when another child enters the picture. Oftentimes, new parents are so distracted with trying to maintain their new routine and take care of the new child, they don't notice when older children are feeling left out. In a perfect world, conversations like this would be had prior to the birth of the new baby so everyone would be better prepared for what to expect and what some specific needs may be. It's really important to focus here on what you do need from your mom when you are with her. Do you want more physical affection, or do you need more time for conversation with her? It's always a good idea to think about what you need instead of thinking about how badly you feel. Ideally, if you can communicate what you feel and what you need, your mom and stepdad will respond well and do what they can to meet those needs or to find a compromise. Multiple conversations to address needs, expectations, and boundaries are usually necessary here. The earlier you share your feelings and needs, the quicker your resentment and disappointment can dissipate.

Q: My dad and stepmom show a lot of affection for each other in front of me, and it makes me really uncomfortable. I never saw my dad and mom showing each other affection, so this is really different for me. Do I just need to get over it?

A: It's normal to feel uncomfortable around displays of affection, especially if you're not used to it. You're trying to accept their new relationship, and it can feel overwhelming to see how close your dad is to your stepmom and wish he had that kind of relationship with your biological mom. Change is hard, and it's important to first notice any emotions that may be present for you. Try to isolate two or three emotions other than just uncomfortable. Learning to label your emotions helps you better understand and connect to yourself. It also helps you better understand what your needs and boundaries might be so you can communicate them more easily. Sometimes noticing another person's show of affection may be a sign that you need affection in a new or different way than you're used to experiencing it. Remember, use opportunities like this to be curious about yourself rather than judgmental of others. There are things that you will learn to adapt to because change has already taken place. Emotions and needs are going to come up when you least expect them. Notice and label each emotion, ask yourself questions about them, and think about if they're something you need to work on internally or if they require a conversation. Maybe both!

Q: I really like my new stepmom, but part of me feels like I'm betraying my mom by building a relationship with her. I'm afraid of making my mom upset, hurt, or jealous. I do spend a lot of time at my dad and stepmom's house, and I really want to make the most of it. What can I do?

A: It's great that you are enjoying the relationship you're building with your stepmom! It's also common to worry about how your biological parent might feel about that relationship. Wanting to be sensitive to your mom is a sign of your maturity. Like you, both of your parents are trying to figure out how all this blended family stuff works and how you feel about it. All of you are in a season of growth brought on by change. Building a relationship with your new stepparent is a healthy and natural thing. If you are worried about how your biological parent might feel, consider talking to them about your fears. Usually they want you to feel safe and comfortable to build a relationship in a way that feels good for you. They may need to do some of their own personal work if they do have big feelings about you developing a relationship with your stepparent. I'll go back to reminding you that change brings grief, and grief brings challenging emotions that we're not always ready or equipped to deal with. You can't avoid hard feelings, and neither can your parents. The goal is to keep staying curious and open to talking about and exploring your feelings and needs.

Q: I barely get to see my half sisters, but I always feel like I'm the one in trouble when they are around. It seems really unfair to me that I'm constantly blamed for things I see them doing. My mom and dad don't want to hear it and think that I'm just trying to get out of trouble. I feel angry and resentful about it, and I don't know how to make things change.

A: I would feel angry and resentful, too, if this were happening to me. Taking personal responsibility for things we do wrong is a sign of growth and maturity, and so is sticking up for ourselves when we feel unjustly punished. It is important that we communicate those feelings. We have to really think about how we're going to say something so that it showcases our truest message. At the end of the day, what do you want to say to your parents, and what do you hope their response will be? Start first with taking responsibility for things you have done to showcase you see your weaknesses and things you can work on. Then share the feelings you have and focus on what can go better next time. For example, "I know that I can be very reactive to Lily and Paige by yelling when they come into my room. I've been really frustrated and easily overwhelmed lately because I need more time to myself with all this change. I need to keep my room private, and I don't want them going in there."

Q: My half brother gets really angry whenever my parents aren't around, and I feel like I have to keep my distance. He will often follow me around and make fun of me. I've tried talking to my parents about it, but because they don't see it happen, nothing changes. This makes me uncomfortable, and I don't want to be left home alone with him anymore. What else can I do?

A: This sounds like a really unsafe situation to me. If you feel unsafe with someone and do not want to be left home alone with them, then you shouldn't have to be. Just because someone doesn't see it happening doesn't mean that it isn't. If you feel like you're in an unsafe situation, talk to a school counselor or another adult who can help you communicate what is going on at home when your parents are not there and set up appropriate boundaries. Do not be afraid to ask for help from other adults in your life if you feel unsafe at home. Feeling comfortable at home is something that everyone deserves. I know that some parents get overwhelmed or believe that something is a phase that will pass, but if you are in danger of your half brother's anger, then he may be needing some support for his emotions as well. Blending your family takes time, but feeling unsafe is not something you should experience in your own home.

Q: I feel sad all the time, like I don't even want to do anything with anyone. My parents have tried talking to me about it, but I don't even know what to tell them. They want some magical answer to make everything better. If I knew the answer, I would tell them. So now I'm just lost, sad, and frustrated. What is wrong with me, and how do I get help if I don't even know what I'm looking for?

A: It is very common for people to feel a certain way frequently and not understand why. This is where trusted adults, friends, and community members (like a pastor, coach, or counselor) can help. Feeling sad all the time is often a sign that there are things you need to process and might need help connecting the dots of your experiences and emotions. It takes a lot of strength to ask for help. Sadness is usually a part of grief when major changes take place in our lives. You may feel like you should be happy, but you just can't get there. Even if you don't know what to say, find someone in your life who you do feel like you can talk to. Find activities that distract you, like your favorite music or show, and use art like drawing, coloring, or painting to express yourself. There is no right way to manage sadness, but overwhelming sadness does require outside support from a trusted source like a therapist, school counselor, pastor, or coach to manage.

A FINAL WORD

You have gone through so much to get to this point. I know it wasn't easy to keep pulling yourself back into difficult emotions and learning new exercises for blending into your new family. There is not a doubt in my mind that implementing a lot of what you learned has come with its own share of pushback and rejection from both yourself and others. Personal growth and development takes time. Just because something didn't work the first time doesn't mean it won't work later on. Much of what I taught you in this workbook requires repetition, consistency, and time to work. Trust me, if there was an easy way through this thing called life, I would have shown it to you! Living life in a blended family may not go as you planned or hoped. You may even wish it had never happened, and the bulk of what you have to do is learn to acknowledge your resistance to change and learn to grieve that change you didn't want.

Whatever stage of this process you're in when it comes to blending your family, know that you are not alone and you will get through this. You will ultimately learn a lot about yourself, your relationships in life, and your dreams or desires for the future. No change is perfect, and oftentimes we have high expectations that reality doesn't match. Allow yourself and others to be the imperfect humans that we all are. Mistakes will be made, things will get tense, but there will also be good moments, too. I will provide you with resources on page 144 for connecting with others or even finding a good counselor if you need one. Don't be afraid to ask for help! Being honest about your feelings is difficult, and stuffing them down will eventually cause more issues. Use the tools in this book to structure new patterns of connecting with your family and yourself!

RESOURCES FOR TEENS

Books

The Blended Family Journal for Teens: Prompts and Practices for Navigating Emotions and Finding Your Way, by Danielle Schlagel

The Mindfulness Journal for Teens: Prompts and Practices to Help You Stay Cool, Calm, and Present, by Jennie Marie Battistin, MA, LMFT

Conquer Negative Thinking for Teens: A Workbook to Break the Nine Thought Habits That Are Holding You Back, by Mary Karapetian Alvord

Websites

NATIONAL STEPFAMILY RESOURCE CENTER

This is a website with links to amazing resources for teens and their families related to tips and tools for blending your family.

StepFamilies.info

PSYCHOLOGY TODAY

If you or your family are needing a local counselor to work through communication struggles, check out this online directory for the names and specialties of counselors in your area.

PsychologyToday.com

TEEN LINE

This is a blog, resources center, and hotline that teens can use for extra support after a divorce or while blending into a new family.

TeenLine.org

Organizations

OUTWARD BOUND

This is a nonprofit organization that seeks to support teens going through difficult times and give them opportunities to have new and exciting adventures.

OutwardBound.org

Mindfulness & Stress-Reduction Apps

CALM

Calm.com

HEADSPACE

Headspace.com

COMBINED MINDS (FREE)

CombinedMinds.co.uk

INDEX

INDEX

ABOUT THE AUTHOR

SONYA JENSEN, LMFT, graduated with honors in 2013 from Azusa Pacific University in San Diego, California. Since graduation, Sonya has gone on to become certified as a Gottman Method couples therapist, sex therapist, and complex trauma professional.

Sonya specializes in treating high-conflict couples and families with complex challenges at her group practice, Sonya Jensen Counseling and Coaching, in Austin, Texas. She is a Licensed Marriage and Family Therapist, relationship coach, author, and speaker who seeks to inspire and educate couples and families with practical and relatable tools.

A candid voice for relationship health, she brings her passion for relationship education to her weekly podcast, *Love and Sex Unfiltered*. You can find her on Instagram and Facebook @thesonyajensen or at her website SonyaJensen.com.

CPSIA information can be obtained
at www.ICGtesting.com
Printed in the USA
JSHW010827240322
24011JS00001B/1